Develop a Positive Mindset and Attract the Life of Your Dreams

Unleash Positive Thinking to Achieve Unbound Happiness, Health, and Success

Richard Banks

Develop a Positive Mindset and Attract the Life of Your Dreams

© Copyright 2020 by Richard Banks. All right reserved
The content contained within this book may not be reproduced, duplicated or transmitted without direct written permission from the author or the publisher.

Under no circumstances will any blame or legal responsibility be held against the publisher, or author, for any damages, reparation, or monetary loss due to the information contained within this book. Either directly or indirectly.

Legal Notice:

This book is copyright protected. This book is only for personal use. You cannot amend, distribute, sell, use, quote or paraphrase any part, or the content within this book, without the consent of the author or publisher.

Disclaimer Notice:

Please note the information contained within this document is for educational and entertainment purposes only. All effort has been executed to present accurate, up to date, and reliable, complete information. No warranties of any kind are declared or implied. Readers acknowledge that the author is not engaging in the rendering of legal, financial, medical or professional advice. The content within this book has been derived from various sources. Please consult a licensed professional before attempting any techniques outlined in this book.

By reading this document, the reader agrees that under no circumstances is the author responsible for any losses, direct or indirect, which are incurred as a result of the use of the information contained within this document, including, but not limited to, — errors, omissions, or inaccuracies.

Introduction 9

Chapter 1: Believing In Yourself 25

Self-knowledge 26

Accept that change happens 56

Summary 58

Chapter 2: The Power of Positive Thinking 61

The History 61

The Present 63

10 Ps for Reprogramming Your Mind 68

Positive energy 78

Summary 99

Chapter 3: Inferiority Complex and Self-Doubt 102

How Inferiority Complex Presents 105

History of the inferiority complex 108

Symptoms and signs of inferiority complex 109

Risk Factors and Causes of Inferiority Complex 115

Dealing with an inferiority complex 119

Summary 126

Chapter 4: Managing Your Emotions 128

What Are Emotions? 128

Why Should You Manage Emotions? 136

Managing Emotions 140

How Does That Connect with a Positive Outlook? 147

Limiting beliefs 151

Summary 174

Chapter 5: Managing Your Relationships 178

Good Relationships? Why? 180

What Makes a Good Relationship? 182

Relationships at Work 184

Ten Tips to Keep Any Relationship Healthy 188

Difficult Relationships 193

Tips for Ending a Bad Relationship 194

Summary 201

Chapter 6: Neuro-Linguistic Programming 205

Dissociation 215

Content Reframing 220

Anchoring Yourself 225

Rapport 231

Persuasion and Influence 237

Summary 243

Chapter 7: Daily Rituals for a Positive Mindset 245

Why Rituals are Important 245

Morning Rituals 250

Before Bed Rituals 257

Summary 269

Chapter 8: Reaching Your Full Potential 272

7 Skills to Reach Your Full Potential 275

Dream, Believe, and Dare to Do 281

Summary 285

Conclusion 288

References 294

Develop a Positive Mindset and Attract the Life of Your Dreams

INTRODUCTION

"Be Positive"- So small a phrase, yet with such magnanimous impact on our lives. Sometimes we wonder, is it really that easy to be positive? Most days, we find ourselves struggling to deal with many problems, some within and some beyond our perception and control. An impending exam result, the responsibility of becoming a father, the untimely loss of a loved one, many problems could arise from the emotional fluctuations you go through in these situations. More often than not, it is highly possible that an individual could ignore the psychological and physical impacts of emotionally intensive scenarios in their life.

This book is my attempt to help you identify problems that you may have been ignoring for quite some time. I have also invested my thoughts and opinions, combined with factual information, to showcase the importance of a positive mindset in solving various problems.

So, what are the problems we are talking about?

- Do you feel stuck in a job or relationship that you don't love anymore?
- Are you struggling to get a comfortable and relaxing night's sleep?
- Have you been feeling like you're missing out on all the fun and enjoyment in your life?
- Are you feeling overwhelmed and need help getting rid of negative thoughts?

- Are you struggling with low self-esteem or a lack of confidence to pursue your dreams?

If you have been experiencing any of these problems, then it is very likely that you are vulnerable to stress, anxiety, and a host of other psychological health issues such as low self-esteem, depression, and little motivation. As these issues develop gradually and manifest themselves in your mind and consciousness, you start feeling burdened by negative thoughts. The overwhelming feeling of negativity building up on your psyche could slowly impair your resolve in life.

Anxiety is a wicked friend. It takes without ever giving back. One thing happens, and before you know it, you are triggered to remember your childhood friend who one time stole your toy or your uncle when he promised a gift that you are still waiting for as an adult. The point is, you begin feeling anxious about one thing, and it gives birth to other things like anger and self-doubt in an unending spiral that only births more places to fall in the pits of despair.

Understandably, when you open a blog post, a newspaper article, or even see your friend's tweet-able advice to just 'think positively,' you might be suspicious and perhaps a little annoyed. You know that optimism is something to strive for, but you also know that it is not that easy.

There is good news.

You do not have to be unrealistic to change

your point of view and become a more positive person.

You must admit to the darker aspects of a particular situation in the process of becoming more positive. Positive thinking is not about denial. It is about having hope and confidence in your ability to deal with the tough things that come at you. It is about remembering that no one thing is all negative every time. In the particularly darker storms of life, you can grab the sunnier takeaways and enjoy the moments of relief, regardless of their size.

If positivity does not naturally come to you, you are more familiar with anxiety than with enthusiasm for life, do not beat yourself up. There are people born with a neural architecture (rose-colored glasses, if you may) that predisposes them to enjoy more positive emotions and to see only the best things in the world. Others come with grey-colored glasses, and that is their genetic lottery.

Before beginning to learn how to be a happier person, you do well to appreciate that wherever you fall, you matter, and the perspective you have to offer is critical, not just for yourself but for everyone around you. That said, it may be challenging for some people more than others to learn to be positive, but everyone can pick up the necessary skills.

Whether you want to leave the daily melancholy behind you and keep confident, or whether you simply want to conquer one area of your life that seems clouded by a shroud of negativity, this book is for you.

Here, you will learn past the commonly touted advice that, although well-intended, can feel empty - things like repeating a personal mantra at yourself or paying little attention to negative thoughts. You will understand the science behind the advice and be able to tailor it to yourself. You will reap the benefits of 'knowledge as power' because after reading through, you will know your 'why,' and as Nietzsche said, that will help you overcome any 'how.'

Say you want to pick a personal mantra. On the first day, you look yourself in the eyes and whisper how beautiful you are, but despite the passion you put to it, something still feels off. You realize that it is not easy to get comfortable with the practice, and any smidge of relief the exercise brings is taken away by the thought of how weird it is. What do you do then?

Or perhaps you want to pay less attention to the negative thoughts you have. You have realized that you get caught up in a loop of concern and worry. You overanalyze everything, and the rumination process causes your mood to plummet even further downward. You congratulate yourself, rightfully so, on the show of progress identifying what the problem is. You resolve to hold things lightly, but that resolve becomes fodder for further over-analysis. Before you know it, you are crippled, in a bad mood, and you do not even remember where it all started. What are you to do?

First, one mistake many people make is assuming that happiness just happens and that you can simply pursue it. However, happiness is a byproduct of being engaged in life. It is not like making money that you foster by analyzing your finances and coming up with an improvement plan. Thinking about making yourself happy will be the first sure sign that it backfires.

Secondly, negative thoughts are not strong enough to control you. You are strong enough to control them. Think of them like TV reruns that you have seen millions of times. Leave them playing in the background and focus on other things. It is a little like telling your mind 'hey, thank you for letting me know,' and then moving your attention elsewhere.

Optimism and a positive outlook are like muscles – the more you train them, the stronger they become.

Research shows that learning to see the half-full glass has many benefits. It can improve the quality of your life and could even extend your lifespan. Researchers at Harvard University studied 70,000 women for eight years. They found that the most optimistic of them had a 30% lower risk of dying from major death causes compared to the less optimistic women (American Journal of Epidemiology, 2016).

If you are not aware of it, positive thinking is not just about your outlook on life. It is also your attitude toward yourself, and that, as experts say, could affect your health. Some studies show that personality traits like pessimism and optimism could affect your wellbeing. Optimism is effective in stress management, which offers numerous benefits to health.

As earlier mentioned, positive thinking is not the equivalent of burying your head in the proverbial sand and ignoring the unpleasant situations. It is about approaching the situations positively and productively – you expect the best to happen, not the worst. It is integrally tied to self-talk.

Self-talk is the constant stream of unspoken thoughts running in your head, which are either positive or negative. Some thoughts are informed by reason and logic, but others come from misconceptions you created because you lacked information. Research shows that if you continuously have negative thoughts, you may be a pessimist.

Research shows that positive thinking leads to:

- Lower depression rates
- Lower distress levels
- Better skills to cope with hardships and stress
- Better heart health
- Reduced risks of death from cardiovascular diseases
- Better physical and psychological wellbeing
- Greater resistance to the common cold

It is not yet clear why there are associations between positive thinking and these health benefits. One of the prevailing theories is that positive thinking will help you better cope with stress and thus reduce the harmful health effects of stress that your body experiences. Another school of thought holds that optimistic people live healthier lifestyles, have healthier diets, and get more physical activity.

Whatever the relation is, the benefits are undeniable, and anyone can potentially enjoy them.

This book will teach you how to identify negative thinking so that you do not just focus on the negative aspects of a situation or blame yourself for bad things that happen.

You will learn how to turn negative thinking into positive thinking and the processes of investing practice and time into forming new habits. You will be able to identify the areas that need changing, live a healthy lifestyle, and talk to yourself in a way that will uplift you.

You cannot expect changes to happen overnight, but with practice, you can learn to criticize yourself less and accept yourself more. This will translate into you being more accepting of the world around you. When your mind is typically optimistic, you can handle whatever comes at you more constructively.

Lao Tzu is recorded as saying to 'watch your thoughts because they become words' (Lao Tzu, 1984). Your words become actions and, in turn, become a habit. Habits become character, and your character shapes your destiny. Otherwise stated, everyone has a set of messages playing over and over in their minds. The personal commentary will influence what you say, do, who you are, your relationships, and eventually your destiny.

There is never a better time to begin working on whatever is dysfunctional in your head than now. Your actions ripple and extend to all the corners of your life. You are part of a network, and how you live life affects the network and spreads to the whole world. A negative approach becomes a self-fulfilling prophecy. You begin to reap what you sow and attract what you are.

Concepts like the law of attraction, birds of a feather flocking together, and attracting what you think all testify to how positive thinking is crucial.

How then do you begin brightening your view of the world and infusing more positivity into the things you think? This book will answer this question and others on the topic. It will empower you to go forth and live a better life. If that sounds like what you care about, keep reading.

Chapter 1: Believing In Yourself

In this chapter, you will learn useful skills for staying positive. For example, how to have faith in your abilities, detoxing your mind, self-confidence, reaching your potential, shifting your mindset, and controlling your thoughts. All these, unless anchored on the correct knowledge, will not last and could quickly become more reasons to be anxious. They have to be based on self-knowledge.

Self-knowledge

The famous philosopher Socrates is believed to have said that the unexamined life is not worth living. When asked what all commandments in philosophy could be whittled down to, he said, 'know yourself.'

Knowing oneself is prestigious in today's culture and has been framed as the meaning of life. It can easily become cliché, so one wonders why self-knowledge is a good thing. What happens if you do not know yourself? How do you come to do it, and why is it so difficult to know oneself?

Self-knowledge refers to a specific kind of knowledge of a psychological or emotional nature. You can know the week that you were born or whether or not you are a morning person but still lack self-knowledge. Not everything you know about yourself is essential to know. Self-knowledge in this section is concerned with your inner psychological core – what kind of person may you be attracted to and why? What are your talents? How are you when you receive feedback? What do you do when life frustrates you?

If you can answer these questions thoroughly, you can speak of yourself as someone who knows themselves well, and you can begin your journey to becoming a positive person.

Think of this process like digging for gold – you have to go deep to find the value. You cannot be afraid to find out what lies beneath the choices you make, the things that cause you to spiral, and your causes for anxiety.

Self-knowledge offers a route to fulfillment and a degree of happiness. If you do not know yourself, you are open to mistaking ambitions. The right knowledge of self gives you more chances for avoiding errors as you deal with others and as you make your life choices.

The main point of this section is to form a basis for reflection before you begin to adopt any of the things this book recommends. That way, you can make the tool entirely yours and ensure that it would be helpful even in the long run.

Have faith in your abilities

At a press conference, Larry Bird once said that

a winner is a person who knows their God-given talents and works to turn them into skills and then uses them to accomplish his goals. The most successful businesspeople in the world are self –confident to the point of coming across as cocky or brash. Consider people like Bill Gates, Donald Trump, and Richard Branson. They have learned not to question their abilities.

Psychologists say one of the ways to become self-confident is to become competent (Kolbert, 2014). There is a straight line between becoming competent at what you do and positive thinking. You will find it easier to see the brighter side of things if you know that you do well at what you put your mind to do. The following are some tips to help you believe in your abilities:

- Focus on your strengths – You know the areas in which you are competent. The skills vary from person to person and from job to job. Pick yours and push yourself hard that you may become even better. You do not want to be mediocre.
- Let things go – It is okay to let some doors close. You cannot do everything, and it is wise not to try. If some things fall off your to-do list, you can delegate and be purposeful in leaving some things out when you need to.
- Take care of yourself – How confident are you when you did not get enough sleep, are always exhausted, and have no energy? Eat right, sleep enough, hydrate, and exercise.
- Wake up early – The old adage 'early to bed, early to rise' is true. It did not earn

its novelty without proving helpful. Many achievers wake up early to spend time meditating, reading, and working without distractions. You can get plenty done when you have some quiet time. Be sure to go to bed early as well.

- Brush up on your skills regularly – Most skills fade over time, more so in the technology and communications sector that is continuously upgrading. Do a personal ROI by continually learning, taking refresher courses, and attending seminars where applicable.

Watch your thoughts

"Life is 10% what happens to you and 90% how you react." — Charles R. Swindoll

Reality is not neutral; you become what you think. You are always passing judgment on the things happening around you. Have you ever been in the same dangerous or risky situation as your friend? What differences did you notice in your responses? Where one helps to find a solution, another may scream and become confused. Where one rallies, another may become crippled with indecision. The point here is that your thoughts and your reality are unavoidably connected. When working to think positively, you have to be aware of this fact.

However, you have to be careful not to make it so simple that it goes against the very thing you are trying to achieve. Positive thinking is not just about the bright side; you have to embrace the whole self. Marcus Aurelius said of the soul that it becomes dyed with the color of the thoughts it has.

The society loves black and white statements that put you in one category and exempt you from another by default. When working to think positively, labels can be a burden.

Everyone has positive and negative thoughts and moments. It can be harmful to always pretend to be happy. If you focus just on one aspect, you will not see your blind spots. As an example, labeling yourself as a negative person could have you overplay your dramas and enter into self-pity.

Researchers say that optimists cope better with stress because they can handle adversity (Schmitz et. al., 2014) not because they always have a positive view. Their immune response is the same as that of pessimists. Positive thinking is not about making all things come true, but about handling all things like a master.

You can only do that if you are able to master yourself. Train yourself to treat your negative thoughts as suggestions from your brain rather than descriptions of who you are. This comes from understanding that there is nothing wrong with having negative emotions.

Positivity is not a status. It is a fluid state. Train your thoughts not to overplay just one aspect of a situation. The trick is to walk the taut line between optimism and pessimism as an observer.

As a rule of thumb, connect to the emotions you have so that you respond instead of react. This looks like not letting your preconceptions to shape how you behave but exploring your emotions so that you understand them. Feed wisdom and compassion instead of anger.

Think of positive thinking as an exercise in self-acceptance. Manage the strengths and flaws that you have to the point where you accept yourself as a person who makes mistakes but is also capable of doing great things. Positive thinking works only if you embrace the full reality of who you are.

Detox your mind

In the world today, attention is currency. The more attention people give something, the more valuable it becomes – the more exposure, the more profit. The more energy you give something, the more it becomes powerful, and in a world that is always asking for your mental energy in emails to answer, clothing to wear, recipes to try, and ways to take photos, you have to guard your mind.

If you do not know what matters most to you, you can easily fall into patterns of anxiety. Unable to understand what deserves space, you can end up wasting your days in rabbit trails. Most people do not realize that you learn and grow from what you experience and absorb consistently. Detoxing your mind is about getting rid of the unnecessary things that make you feel burdened and stand in the way of you embracing a positive outlook on life.

The following are tips for detoxing your mind:

- Make a list of what to worry about

Have you ever noticed that if you have a plan for solving a problem, you no longer need to worry about it? The idea is simple; you do not worry about issues because you think rumination on them is productive. You worry about making sure you do not forget to deal with the issue because it is risky, or the threat it poses is huge.

Write everything down that bothers you in a 'to worry about' list. Set time aside so that you can review that list. You will find that most of the fears you have are unfounded, and you can make a plan to deal with the ones you can handle.

- Adopt junk journaling

Take a notebook and devote it only to things

that you can classify as 'junk.' Keep the journal safe and private. Anytime you feel worked up, or your mind begins spinning, write everything down that comes to mind. Release the thoughts you have even if they do not make sense or you do not truly believe them.

- Spend time outside

Research has proven that when people spend more time in nature, they begin to see significant benefits to their health and wellness. Spending time in nature also allows you an easy way to gain clarity and to relax. You need that to put things into perspective.

- Unfollow those who do not add to your life

In a world where social media is almost a need,

one can get caught up in a rabbit hole and find themselves without even realizing it in a cycle of comparisons and negative self-talk. Make a point of spending time filtering who you allow on your social media. If you spend time online, you might as well make it positive and productive. Assess who you follow regularly and ensure that every account you follow is actively adding to your life.

- Clean out old phone numbers

Everyone has some people that you know you will never speak to again or *should* never speak to again. It is part of being human. You want to allocate some time to delete any old phone numbers. This is not even about getting rid of temptation even if that could be part of it – bye, bye pesky ex – this is about the feeling you get after removing things you do not need. You will remember how far you have come, and everyone needs a dose of gratitude. It will also inject you with a sense of closure.

- Clear out your inbox

Your inbox should be like a 'to do' list. What is in your inbox every day should tell you what you need to attend to. Nothing is more stressful than fearing that you have lost important messages in your account because you do not have it cleaned out.

- Unsubscribe from unnecessary promotional information and emails

It could be that at one point you needed a service and you have outgrown it. Or perhaps, you subscribed to support a friend. Other times you even subscribe by mistake. Whatever the case, you may be prone to scrolling on websites every time you see a sale, and that could be eating into your time or expenses. As part of keeping your inbox clean and saving money and time, unsubscribe from anything you do not need. As a rule of thumb, set time to do a major cleaning of your inbox. From there, make a note to delete and unsubscribe from anything you do not want the first time you see it so that they do not pile up.

- Figure out the time you spend online

Research shows that many young people spend up to four hours online consuming content they do not even like. Imagine spending four hours every day, for two months, for example – assuming that you do not go online on weekends, which is highly unlikely; you spend up to seven days online in two months. It is tragic if that time is not spent doing productive things.

Download a browser extension to record how much time you spend online and on what sites you spend that time. Take an honest look at the number. There are also other downloadable apps on your phone that could track your time on social media. If that number is shocking to you, you know that it is time to change.

- Take a day off without photographs

You can live your life without having to document it. In today's era, it is possible to document and share all parts of your life online, which could expose you to security risks and could also introduce a pressure, making you feel like you have to constantly 'perform.' This may create undue stress, more so when you start making choices based on how you would appear to people instead of how the decisions would feel to you.

- Reflect on your life

If you did not know how your life looked to other people, how would you feel about it? Ask yourself this question honestly and find the areas of your life that you are genuinely happy with. Get rid of the parts you only enjoy because of the way they make you look to other people.

- Make it hard to sign in to social media

As earlier discussed, you can spend plenty of

time mindlessly scrolling through social media. If you decide that that is not something you want any more for your life, you can make it more difficult to access social media accounts. You can remove the auto-save option for your passwords, or you can delete the apps from your phone. Either way, make social media apps less accessible.

- Watch how you socialize

Personalities affect much of the way people socialize with others (Jung, 1921). A classic trait of ambiverts is that they are social and outgoing in some settings. This is a critical habit for anyone to develop regardless of where they fall on the extrovert – introvert scale. Be mindful of who you spend time with, what you share with them, who you connect with, and how you vent.

This can affect your wellbeing, your life, and who you become.

- Remind yourself what the big picture is

What are your long-term goals? You want to set aside time to note what those goals are and call it a life vision. Reference this vision often and always have it in mind as you do the mundane tasks of life. It is easy to be caught up in the small details of life without knowing why. When you understand why, you can make supporting decisions that will lead you to your goal.

- Protect your mental space as much as you can

There is a common saying that asserts, 'There is nothing that enters a man from outside which can defile him, but the things which come out of him, those are the things that defile a man.' This idea is echoed in many sayings like 'do not judge a book by its cover' or 'still waters run deep.' Undeniably, what you let into your heart is what will make you the kind of person you become. If you are always listening to gossip, you will likely begin to enjoy no other form of conversation.

As part of de-cluttering your mind, be vigilant about protecting what you hear. Shift the conversation with friends who always gossip. Watch news selectively so that you do not stress yourself out with things you have no control over. The idea here is to commit to being the most peaceful and grounded person that you can be. Do not let just anything grab and keep your attention.

Shifting your mindset

At this point, if you have observed the tips on detoxing your mind, you have a lot of mental energy left to give to whatever it is that you choose. You will notice that you feel lighter. That is good. It means that you are headed in the right direction.

In life, change is inevitable, and you have to learn to accept it and maybe even anticipate it without making it a major mental hurdle. Chances are, as you did the suggested exercises, some things became clearer, and you realized things you do not need.

In this section, you will learn how to stay in this frame of mind with simple mental exercises.

You do not want to slip back into mindless activities. It is a truth of today's generation that more people go through life mindlessly in one area or another. Shifting your mindset, in this case, refers to cementing some of the things you have learned about yourself as you detoxed your mind. The following are things you can do:

- Meditate

Mindset is a muscle that can be improved upon and strengthened. One way to do this is to learn meditation. You do not have to be on the Alps with white garb and spend three months as a monk to learn how to do this. To get you started, when you find your thoughts wandering, remind yourself of the big picture you formulated. Mull over it and always find practical ways to make it a reality. You can commit to doing this for ten minutes a day for starters.

- Prioritize personal development

If you are reading this book, it says a lot about your composition and desire for change. You can zoom in on this desire. Making personal development a priority is about always pausing to find out where you are in life and the changes you need to make. Self-inquiry is at the heart of this.

- Notice three positive changes every day

Dopamine is a feel-good neurotransmitter that the brain releases when you engage in activities like sex or other enjoyable things. It contributes to feelings of satisfaction or pleasure as part of the reward system. You can make sure you enjoy such feelings every day by noticing three changes in your life that are a result of your efforts. However small, make an effort to note them, and you will retrain your brain for growth.

- Write a post-mortem

Positive emotions are excellent and propelling, but sometimes you need something to run away from so that you can keep yourself moving forward. The idea here is to imagine the worst-case scenario for your life. Do not play about with it. Ask yourself what you can imagine to be the worst possible future for yourself and spell it out. Once you realize how simple it is for a person to mess up their life, you will be quick to embrace change.

- Imagine the inevitable

"The only certainty in life is death" – Benjamin Franklin.

There is wisdom in occasionally contemplating death and imagining what kind of legacy you would like to leave. Once you know that this life is fleeting, you can position yourself to make changes instead of being stagnant when you encounter something you do not like. Imagine for a minute that you were writing your eulogy; what would you want to be said about you? If you find that 'he was a kind man' is something you would desire, use that as a springboard. On days you feel less than motivated, ask yourself what you would do differently if you learned that this was the last day of your life, and then do that.

- Enhance your inner work

Earlier in the book, it was mentioned that self-acceptance has one of the foundational truths of positive thinking. Inner work is a pillar of self-acceptance. Inner work is the spiritual and psychological practice of diving deep into your inner self for the purpose of self-exploration, self-understanding, healing, and transformation.

Every person has some things about them that they could improve. It is easy to demand that people accept you for who you are, and there is a sense to which loved ones must do this, but successful people are those who learn to master themselves.

To do this, listen to trusted loved ones. They may not know you the way you know yourself, but their outsider perspective can help you to understand what areas to focus on to lead you out of the 'mental quicksand.' Be honest with yourself, and you will begin to see the results.

Inner work also goes beyond listening to your loved ones (Johnson, 1986). It is about illuminating your hidden feelings, thoughts, memories, beliefs, wounds, prejudices, shadows, and other emotional or mental conditions that influence your ability to feel whole at your core. Doing inner work is about moving past your limitations, fears, addictions, loneliness, depressions, and feelings of un-wholeness that are common to human beings but unique to each person, their experiences, and perception of the world.

The following are some signs you need to enhance inner work:

- You feel lost
- You have people-pleasing tendencies
- You do not know who you are
- You feel like an outsider in the world no matter how hard you try
- Life feels unreal
- You are not confident being who you are
- You frequently get into fights
- You are constantly unmotivated
- You have low self-esteem
- You feel a sense of hopelessness
- You have fits of intense sadness or anger
- You struggle to trust other people
- You self-sabotage
- You feel a sense of emptiness
- You are unable to sleep properly

- You keep attracting the wrong people in your life
- You keep repeating mistakes
- You have many and strong emotional triggers
- You get easily obsessive and neurotic

Ideally, everyone should assess their inner work two or three times a year to recalibrate, stay on track, and get rid of any emotional baggage they may have picked up along the way. The more signs you relate with, the more it points to a need to do inner work first.

Think of this practice as a foundational principle for positive thinking. It is akin to digging deep into the ground when building a house so that it stands firm. Thereafter, think of it as maintenance.

Accept that change happens

Three things are true for every person regardless of their situation in life: time is precious, life is short, and your ego always needs some humility. Whether it is an innovative idea or a business venture, the nature of life is evolution. Change is as natural as oxygen. You need to accept that. You need to recognize also that change will happen with your help or without it, and you get to choose which option it will be.

If you want to make sure that you are party to the changes happening in your life and around you, be vulnerable and open to those around you, and accept their help with discretion.

Accepting change is the path of least resistance, but sometimes it may not be the best path. Only a community can help you to understand when to let go and when to resist. You do not need to let everyone you meet in, but if you accept the thoughts of other people you value, you not only shift your mindset, but you also become a better person in whatever capacity you have to operate.

Get rid of the 'sunken cost mindset.' This is the idea that you have invested so much time in something and so you need to stay attached to it. Sometimes walking away or pivoting is the better decision. Do not allow the fear of losing your investments be what guides your choices. Think rationally about what you get from continuing down a path or going a new direction.

Summary

Nurture your mind with great thoughts, for you will never go any higher than you think." - Benjamin Disraeli

Let's recap the things you have learned by this point:

Positive thinking is a bit more than a fad. For it to be successful, you have to think of it as an exercise in changing who you are at your core in some ways. It is about:

- Knowing yourself
- Having faith in your abilities
- Watching your thoughts
- Detoxing your mind
- Shifting your mindset
- Accepting that change happens

Develop a Positive Mindset and Attract the Life of Your Dreams

Develop a Positive Mindset and Attract the Life of Your Dreams

Chapter 2: The Power of Positive Thinking

The History

The term 'positive thinking' has been in use for a while, but few people know where it comes from. It has religious roots, but it does not come from one religion. Positive thinking has evolved from all religions of the world through a new thought movement. One Harvard professor and psychologist wrote about the movement when writing about the varieties of religious experience. He referred to it as the religion of a healthy mind saying that the most significant discovery of his generation was that man could change his life by changing the attitude of his mind.

New thought originated in Europe in the 1700s, and then later, Ralph Waldo Emerson introduced it to the United States. He focused on perception, saying that moods, temperaments, and thoughts color reality. In a famous essay, he wrote that temperament is the 'iron wire on which you string beads' (Emerson, 1841). He said that life is about moods arranged like beads in a string and that people pass through them, proving to have many lenses to paint their world their hue.

It was not enough to talk about truth, according to Emerson. Words alone could never make people see their own temperament. In his preaching, Emerson stirred people up and inspired a different breed of poets and writers who subscribe to the new thought.

There are countless examples of people who have done amazing things based on changing how they view life. A Hindu guru, Swami Vivekananda, founded the Vedanta society at the height of the positive thinking movements. The common thread with all the examples is the power of thought. Everyone agrees that 'whatever you think, so are you.'

The Present

The power of positive thinking is remarkable. You may still believe that the idea that your mind could change your world is too good to be true, but be assured that there is a lot of good you derive from thinking positively.

Before getting into the nitty-gritty of changing how you think, can you guess the things the most successful people think about all day every day?

It is simple: healthy and happy people mull over the things they want and how to get them. When you consider and talk about the things you want and how to get them, you feel more in control of your life and happier. You trigger your brain to release endorphins that directly improve your mood and, consequently, your perception.

Optimism

Psychological tests show that happy people appear to have a unique quality that makes them live a better life than the average person. They are optimistic. The best news about it is that you can learn to be optimistic. It's a mindset.

By the law of cause and effect, if you say and do what other happy and healthy people with a positive attitude say and do, you will soon become one of them, see the same results, and have similar experiences.

Optimists have a way of seeing things differently as they interact with the world. They keep their minds on the things they want and ways to get it. Their goals are clear, and they are confident that they will get to them eventually.

Optimists also try to find the good in every situation or problem. It is a truth universally acknowledged that if you are looking for something beneficial or good in a situation or a person, you will ultimately find it.

Optimists also look to find the lesson in every failure or setback. Instead of blaming other people and getting upset, they control their emotions. They ask the question, what can I learn from this experience? Emotion control is a major aspect of positive thinking, which is why it gets a chapter of its own later in the book.

You can decide today that you will develop a positive attitude toward yourself and a positive way of thinking about your life and the people around you. From there, you have to train your mind to focus on one thought at a time until you form neural pathways that establish new habits.

It is difficult to change your way of thinking in the heat of the moment when emotions are running high. In one sense, positive thinking is about a decision you make in advance. You have to decide that whatever comes at you, you will strive to respond positively. You will look to help as opposed to making things worse.

As a general rule, happy people are grateful for what they have in life instead of complaining or worrying about what they do not have.

Assume that people around you mean well. Most people are decent and are doing the best that they know how to. Look for the good in their actions and words, and you will surely find it in the words they tell you or in the ways they choose to behave. With that as a background, resolve that you will be cheerful regardless of the circumstance.

In actuality, it is easy to be cheerful when things go as you plan, but what about when you are dealing with challenges and setbacks?

After learning how to think positively, you will start to notice many exciting changes in your environment. Your brain will start running on endorphins that will boost your confidence, and you will feel more capable of meeting challenges and doing greater things outside of your comfort zone. How then do you do that?

10 Ps for Reprogramming Your Mind

In one way or another, most people are not

living the life of their dreams and may have settled into the status quo.

If you have a vague idea of the things you think you deserve and are feeling frustrated because you veered off the path, you can use the discontentment as fuel to reprogram your mind and change. Discontentment, though, is double-edged. Without proper handling, your frustration could sabotage your potential instead of helping it. Most people will work hard for a few days and then revert to their old ways instead of making a lasting change.

Controlling your mind and redirecting your focus on making the life you want is a sure way to make sure you live a life that will give you passion, joy, and fulfillment. Your brain is meant to regulate and reinforce your life.

There is a homeostatic impulse in your mind that regulates functions like breathing, heartbeat, and temperature. Through that autonomic nervous system, the homeostatic impulse maintains a balance of brain chemicals and helps your body function in harmony most times. What you may not realize is that your brain is meant to regulate your physical self and tries to regulate your mental self as well. It is continuously bringing things to your attention and filtering others out. No wonder you may encounter stimuli to reaffirm your existing beliefs. Psychologists refer to this as confirmation bias. You may then have repeated impulses and thoughts which mirror and mimic the things you did in the past.

In that sense, your subconscious acts as a gatekeeper for your comfort zone. It is the realm where you stay habitually and represents everything you expect and the actions you routinely build and reinforce. When you want to change your way of doing things, whether it is in just one area or a complete change, here are a few tips:

1. Prepare for unobvious change

Often when people talk about positive thinking, they make the connection between thinking positively and the belief that you have the ability to do something. While that is true, the first step to creating a significant change is not believing it to be possible, but being willing to see if it could be.

You cannot expect to make the jump from a full-on skeptic to a totally sold out believer. The step into being open to the possibilities is a major one at the beginning. Perhaps you are trying to do a task you have been postponing for months, or maybe it is a scary email proposition you need to send. Whatever the case, the first step to reprogramming your mind is seeing if you are willing to see the change you hope for as a possibility.

2. Permit yourself to succeed

Rather than regurgitating the old story that has kept you from doing the task at hand in the first place, you can change your inner monologue to something like, 'I allow my life to be good.'

Permit yourself to be successful and happy without feeling guilty about it. Most people will find that they have associations between being dishonorable or corrupt and success. If you are one such person, you may need to work harder than you expect. Consider the chapter on managing emotions.

3. Process other people's fears

Have you ever told your friend news you found exciting, and they responded with a simple, 'oh'? Sometimes what feels to you to be a feat could be unimpressive in the eyes of another person. Part of reprogramming your mind is remembering that people's fears are projections of whatever their situations are. They say nothing to your capability. When you encounter such fears, sit with them and process them in a journal, for example, and then let them go.

4. Positively reinforce yourself

Positive reinforcement could be anything that works for you. It could be a champagne bottle in the fridge for celebrations, or it could be making your morning alarm call to congratulate you. The idea here is to make sure that whatever you touch brings hopefulness and positivity. You can even keep post-it notes in your mirror or computer – whatever improves your perception of your worth is worth doing.

5. Profess your present success

It may be a bit of a stretch to say statements like 'I am a CEO' or 'I own a yacht' before they are a reality. Still, you do want to start speaking about the things you want out of life and not in terms of something to do in the future. Rather than saying, 'I hope to accomplish this...' say instead that, 'I am working towards this...' Do not make the mistake of thinking that you will be happy when you meet your goal, but strive for happiness as you work towards it.

6. Perfect your vision space

Earlier in the book, you learned to create a life goal and to keep it in mind. On this point, you want to write it on paper and have it somewhere you can easily see it. Whether it is a Pinterest board, a notebook, a blog, or words in a journal, you want a representation of your goal to bring up whenever you need some more motivation.

7. Pinpoint your resistance

Your subconscious will sometimes hold you

back because you have conflicting beliefs. To identify your beliefs, answer the questions highlighted under the chapter on mastering your emotions. Find a way to meet the needs that cause you to procrastinate before you move forward.

8. Plan your life

This point is set separately from your vision space because there is more to it. It is difficult to make an accurate ten-year plan. Things keep changing over time. For example, before you learn a new skill, you could only be qualified for two jobs. After learning, you are eligible for five more, and your options increase. The better you become in one aspect, the more likely that you will have more and better choices.

Planning your life is about identifying your motivations and your core values. What ultimate goal do you want to meet while you are alive? What legacy do you want to leave behind? These are the things that should guide every decision you make in life.

9. Present your requests

Ask for the things you want, even if there is a chance of being denied. If you are looking for a promotion in your workplace, sit with your boss and announce your intentions. Reach out to other companies. Begin asking for the things you want, and eventually, you will start to get them.

10. Proceed with the flow

Your job is to focus on the 'what' and not get

caught up on the 'how.' If you want, for example, to be able to run your business remotely, rather than giving up when your first attempt fails, reimagine other ways to achieve that vision that are more financially lucrative.

The point is that you cannot predict life – it will surprise you the way things get accomplished. Rather than obsessively attaching to all the details working out as you expect they should, open yourself to the possibilities and potential even if they present ideas you never thought of before.

Positive energy

You have probably heard this phrase in the world of social media often used interchangeably with 'positive vibes.' It is all about controlling the things you think about.

You create and experience different kinds of energies that affect the way you feel and what you do. Some energies are powerful and easy to recognize, and others are subtle and intuitively felt. It is fair to say that everything you sense is energy.

The things that you think, say, and do, even the things you do not do, produce an energy that will affect you and those around you. If you concentrate on producing positive energy, you will begin to see your life improve, and you will touch more lives than you ever imagined.

So what exactly is energy?

Think of energy as anything that will invoke a reaction inside you – if it makes you react, feel, ponder, or tick, that is energy. It comes to people in different forms. The seat you take in the morning, the music you choose to listen to, and the book you are just starting to read all provoke some reaction inside of you.

Consider music; how does your favorite kind make you feel? What energy do you get from it? If you are still not clued in on what energy is about, take out your music player and play a song you like. Take a break from reading this book, close your eyes, and pay attention to the song as it plays. What do you feel?

Music is among the most easily recognizable and powerful forms of energy. No wonder it formed the basis of many traditions. An excellent musician has the ability to create sensations in the audience.

If you want to shift your energy quickly, music is one of the easiest ways. Athletes will often listen to songs before they go to play to channel their adrenaline; artists often play music to get "in the zone," and many writers will rely on music in their writing process.

However, even though music is the simplest way to explain the concept, it is not the only way to get energized.

Some people wake up, swing open the curtains, and allow the sun in as the first thing and draw energy from that. Other people run to coffee. On the reverse, some people find rain to have the potential to affect their mood negatively, so they find it beneficial to practice mindfulness when it is raining.

The most important thing about feeling positive energy is being fully present. When you are in the moment, you will be able to respond in ways that are truly you and that propel you forward.

Still, it may not be as simple as A-B-C-D. To help obtain positive energy, you can make a list of everything that makes you feel good and use it as a basis for the things to do when your mood is off. If you find that being in nature gives you that energy, you can try spending some more time in the outdoors. If the sun does that for you, there is a chance that animals, trees, and flowers will do the same. This is discussed further in the chapter on daily rituals.

The benefits

Positive energy is contagious. If you are the kind of person that emits positivity and zeal, the outer world will begin to notice.

Do you know of people that everyone likes to be around? These are people who radiate alluring energy all the time, and everyone loves to feed off that energy. They make other people smile with their stories and with their attitudes.

It is indeed challenging to keep positive energy flowing in an unwaveringly cynical world.

The unpredictability of life often causes people to have volatile emotions. Everyone experiences emotional ups and downs as life unfolds. If you do not know how to process those experiences, you will leave some emotions unresolved in an emotional bypass. For example, one of the driving ideas of positive energy is the ability and the space to process emotion and deal with it in healthy ways, before you are consumed by it. It assumes that while your circumstances can change at any time and have a degree of mystery to them, your inner world does not have to be the same.

If your ability to deal with the stresses of everyday life is underdeveloped, you run the risk of having a negative outlook on life by default. Undoubtedly, negativity will manifest as stress, and when you are stressed, you put yourself at risk emotionally, mentally, and physically. To counteract stress and thus the negative energy, you have to be proactive in understanding your thoughts and behaviors that cause the negative cycle.

Positive energy will bring you the following benefits:

- Improving your relationships

Relationships are a vital part of life. If they are strong, they will strengthen you and can make you more energetic and happier. Relationships with a strong bond based on positivity will often last the longest and will serve you the best.

- Becoming a more spiritual person

Positivity supports your spirituality. Spiritual people believe in something higher than themselves as they go through life. They draw strength from spiritual connectivity and faith. Studies show that spiritual people are mentally stronger and cope with stress better.

- Unleashing your creativity

Positive energy will boost your creativity. It will

make you more likely to find innovative solutions to your problem. Some famous people say that their positivity kept them going because it encouraged them to think outside the box. Your solution-finding becomes child-like.

- Feeling more relaxed

Stress can harm your body and mind. It takes away your energy and puts you on edge. Boosting your positive energy will make you relax and equip you to deal with the difficulties that come your way.

- Improving your sleep

Positive energy has both physical and mental benefits. According to a study that looked to understand the relationship between sleep and positivity, researchers found that positivity helps a person to sleep soundly. It lessens insomnia related to stress. Negative people are prone to worry, and worry eats at your mind at times when you are supposed to be resting. If you can sleep well, your immune system will run better; you will have better heart health, breathing, and lower blood pressure, all of which contribute to a better quality of life.

- Improving productivity

Positivity will give you the energy you need to do the things you need to do. Fear can steal from your strength and negatively influence your productivity. Positive energy will unburden your mind to make you feel ready to tackle whatever comes your way.

- Giving you an attitude of gratitude

Positive energy will boost your general view of life. Researchers say that a happy attitude almost always leads to a happy life. Positive energy helps to take a step back and see the blessings you have in life and to be grateful for them.

- Being a better role model

If you are a parent, you know that nothing would make you happier than to see your children become successful and mature adults. Positive energy will help you model the kind of life you would want your kids to lead one day. They will see the way you handle difficulties, and they will learn from you.

- Improving self-confidence

Positive energy is inevitably tied to self-confidence. It will strengthen your resolve to deal with the difficult things in life. It will help you to fight fear, which can be paralyzing when you want to try new things.

The roadblocks and how to overcome them

Everyone can enjoy the benefits of positive thinking, but not everyone manages to. The following are some of the roadblocks that could get in the way and how you can overcome them:

- Letting success dictate your life

It is normal to desire success, and that is not negative behavior. However, the obsessive preoccupation with that success, which then commands and directs your life, is unhealthy. This is the reason many successful people are miserable.

Allowing society to influence what success means to you is toxic. Society is often consumer-based and materialistic, and so its definition of success may be based on how much money you have in your bank account, the home you live in, and the car you drive. This definition does not allow for the uniqueness of individuality.

To address this, you have to re-define what success means to you and keep your focus on your life vision and what truly brings you happiness. Envision what a successful life looks like to you and resolve to live it without letting outside influences in.

- Preoccupation with self-image or vanity

Joan Rivers, a very talented comedian, actress, and television host, was famously known for being obsessed with the way she looked and underwent more than 730 plastic surgeries in her life. She continued with the procedures until she died at 81.

You may not think of yourself as someone who would go to such an extent but think about it. In what ways have you bought into the society's definitions of beauty – expensive makeup, makeovers, toned bodies, fancy hairstyles, and designer clothes? Most young people will find themselves susceptible to these influences. You can see this in disorders like anorexia and bulimia, which often lead to depression and even suicide.

Trying to be accepted and to improve your self-image by going by what society calls beauty will prove empty. True beauty can only be found in your mind, heart, and soul. Recognize and love yours.

- Addiction to stress

Believe it or not, studies have shown that some people are addicted to stress.

"We wear our stress like a badge of honor, humble-bragging about how little sleep we got last night, how our weekend was spent racing to meet a deadline, and how we're too busy to take a vacation." – Nuwer, Rachel (2014)

The psychological repercussions of ongoing stress include headaches, increased heart rate, asthma, obesity, depression, and diabetes, among others.

Stress addiction does not come from external circumstances but your internalization of stress. The solution to this is deep breathing, guided imagery, and meditation. Practice the daily morning and evening rituals discussed in the final chapter if you are prone to this.

- Worrying about the mundane in life

I recently stumbled across an interesting post on social media: "Imagine if you had $86,400 in your account, and someone stole $10 from you. Would you be upset and throw away the remaining $86,390 in hopes of getting back at the person who took your $10? Or would you just move on and live? We all have 86,400 seconds each day. Don't let someone's negative

10 seconds ruin your remaining 86,390."

It is annoying to run five minutes late for a meeting, and it's an inconvenience to forget your cell phone at home. However, these are not significantly life-changing issues. Why would you allow them to derail your mood?

It is alright to get irritated when the small and unpleasant event happens, but do not become overindulgent. You are merely wasting time and energy on situations that are insignificant and trivial. It can lead to unwarranted stress and anxiety. Don't sweat the small stuff. Let thoughts fade before they become a negative mindset.

- Living in the past

Regardless of the severity and number of

mistakes you've made in the past, every day is a second chance. It is impossible to live in the moment when you continuously replay and reflect on the past. Continually replaying the mistakes of the past will condition your brain to always expect the worst. It becomes counterproductive to the future and the present, and you begin to feel burdened and victimized.

There are times it may be hard to just 'forget and move on,' especially if you experienced trauma, but it is not impossible. Consider meditation and journaling to help you in the process of healing.

- Possessiveness in your relationships

When you are possessive, you cling tightly to

people and relationships, saying 'mine!' Possessiveness is a sure sign of fear and insecurity. It could be coming from conditioning, but possessiveness harms you and your loved ones. It breeds problems like loneliness, anxiety, sadness, and anger, which compromise your sense of understanding and peace. More often than not, it yields a result opposite to what you want – disconnection from your loved ones.

The first step to dealing with possessiveness is thinking of protecting the people you care for from yourself. Everyone needs freedom and space to make choices that are good for them. Accept that fact and realize that distance may actually strengthen the relationship.

- Unforgiveness

Forgiveness is often considered the first step to healing. Unfortunately, some people nurse grudges for long periods. That unrelenting bitterness will cause anger and resentment to build, which will ultimately disrupt your positive energy. It will make it harder to manage your emotions and establish healthy relationships.

To deal with this, remember that when you forgive someone, it is as much about you as it is about them. Let go, and you will be able to embrace gratitude, joy, hope, and peace. You will lessen the psychological and emotional impact of the hurt. Forgiveness will not excuse or justify their actions, but it will help you to make peace.

- Judging others

There are times you may judge someone's motive from merely looking at them. On the one hand, not judging others can be counterproductive and harmful – it is reasonable to evaluate and observe others to know how to conduct yourself around them. On the other hand, judging others could be damaging when specific feelings or thoughts cause resentment.

When you have a negative perception, you will likely become dismissive or hostile. When you start to feel this way, remind yourself of the path you are walking and ask yourself questions like: Why do I judge them? Do I understand how they think? Can I be empathetic in this situation? Do I know what they are dealing with?

Summary

In this chapter, you have learned that positive thinking is not just a fad that began yesterday. Its roots trace far back into history. In deciding to embrace a positive mindset, you have decided to join a community of many highly regarded people in history. You have also chosen a healthier life with the numerous benefits of having a positive mindset.

Practice the ten **P's** to reprogram your mind. **P**repare for change, **P**ermit yourself to be happy, **P**rocess your emotions, **P**ositively reinforce yourself, remembering that you are your biggest fan, and **P**rofess your beliefs. As you do so, make sure that your vision is **P**erfect and that you have **P**inpointed what often gets in your way. **P**lan your life according to your core values, **P**resent your requests to the right people and **P**roceed with the flow.

You will soon see yourself dealing with the challenges of living better. When you encounter problems, as you inevitably will, come back to the section on roadblocks and find out how to overcome things like:

- Judging others
- Unforgiveness
- Possessiveness in relationships
- Stress addiction
- Living in the past and
- Worrying about the mundane in life

Develop a Positive Mindset and Attract the Life of Your Dreams

Chapter 3: Inferiority Complex and Self-Doubt

Everyone, at some point, questions their abilities. Even though it is distressing, it is normal that one would wonder whether they measure up to other people. It is also reasonable to momentarily feel incompetent for maybe performing less than you expected or for not being as well-situated in life as others.

However, those feelings of insufficiency and insecurity are supposed to be occasional or situational. When they arise, you may brood over them for a short while and then move on by reminding yourself that you have other strengths. Even when a major event causes a flare in self-doubt, you would preferably find ways to feel secure, engaged, and productive.

This is often harder for people who have an inferiority complex. This is an old-fashioned term for chronic low self-esteem. People with an inferiority complex will not bounce back as quickly. You may lament your shortcomings, call yourself names, and criticize yourself harshly, attacking your self-esteem when it is most fragile. The cycle can be so deep that it holds you back professionally and personally.

People who have low self-esteem tend to get very little because they expect little. It becomes a self-fulfilling divination, so as disappointments mount, you become more vulnerable and discouraged, and you become biased against yourself. Consequently, you reinforce the feelings of being 'less than' in many aspects of life – physically, intellectually, psychologically, and socially.

The good news is that there are things you can do to deal with the unhealthy responses and to get over the psychological distress that may stand in the way of you being positive. There are ways to build your self-esteem. Before considering those, let's discuss what inferiority complex looks like:

How Inferiority Complex Presents

Having the assurance that Usain Bolt would outrun you in a sprint is not the same as having a feeling of being inferior. An inferiority complex is the constant and unyielding feeling that you have to measure up to everyone else. It is ungrounded in reality, because all you know is that you do not measure up, but you cannot identify why.

Inferiority complex or low-self-esteem is a generalized feeling of inadequacy whose basis is not rational judgment.

The following is a list of emotions that people with a low self-esteem commonly experience:

- Helplessness and hopelessness – These are critical emotions for someone who is depressed as well. You feel that no matter what you do, you cannot be as good as you should be or as other people appear to be. Regardless of how well you do it, it will not be good enough. It is common for some high achievers to still feel like they are failures.

- Anxiety – In this case, you fear being unmasked or found out to be inadequate. It may also have a sense of imposter syndrome even when you are doing well in different areas of life.
- Resentment, defensiveness, and envy – You can experience envy, resentment, and defensiveness so frequently that you become unable to tell them apart. They sometimes accompany guilt.

My friend, Caroline, often said that she felt

'ugly.' Objectively speaking, she was not, but that did not matter. Felling ugly and being ugly can be disconnected. In that frame of mind, evidence of the objective perception of others is often rejected and rationalized away – it has to be so that the inferiority complex protects itself.

Caroline then continues to rehearse the narrative that she is not good enough. She soon finds it hard to be specific even though she tries to articulate her feelings and where they come from. Where do you think her inferiority complex came from?

Think about this example as you read the rest of this chapter and try to answer it at the end based on what you learn.

History of the inferiority complex

The APA (American Psychological Association) defines the term 'inferiority complex' as the basic feeling of insecurity and inadequacy one feels from imagined or actual psychological or physical deficiencies.

The term was coined in 1907 by an influential psychoanalyst Alfred Adler. He used it to explain why many people do not have the motivation to do what is in their best interests and to pursue the goals they have in life.

Contemporary psychologists, psychiatrists, and mental health professionals use the term interchangeably with low self-esteem.

Symptoms and signs of inferiority complex

As earlier mentioned, it is human nature to sometimes feel inferior, but the key is in how you respond to those feelings.

Do the feelings of inferiority motivate you to try and do better and to learn? They should. Or do they cause you to shut down and distrust? Worse still, do you get jealous of other people and put them down to make yourself feel better? Do you blame others for things you should work to change? When patterns like these become consistent in many circumstances, you may have an inferiority complex.

It will show up as a collection of negative feelings, thoughts, tendencies, and behaviors.

The following are signs to look out for:

- Perfectionism

In this case, one overcompensates to make up for whatever makes them feel inadequate. A person could try to achieve more and to be perfect in whatever they do. Sometimes, they become cocky as they present their achievements to the point where they sound narcissistic.

- You prefer fading into the background

Inferiority complex is closely linked to avoidant behavior. For example, you feel comfortable being overlooked, or you avoid stepping up in social situations because you are afraid of being rejected. It could get to the place where other people notice your discomfort with yourself.

- Sensitivity to criticism

People with low self-esteem are incredibly susceptible to the thoughts of others and will take offense even when it is unintended. Any kind of criticism or critique is held and ruminated over. They will not respond kindly to jokes or teasing at their expense, and when they feel disrespected, they take out aggression on others to intimidate them and to reduce the feelings of being attacked.

- Fault finding

When you have low self-esteem, you may make a habit of finding other people's faults. You tend to be more critical of other people. If a friend appears to be more successful than you are, you may look down on their career path instead of being happy for them. Some people even take it further still, bullying others and putting them down consistently.

- You only like yourself when you outshine others

Comparison is human nature, but there are unhealthy and healthy ways to deal with it. The healthy way is to focus on making yourself a better person. If you have an inferiority complex, you focus on being better than others.

- You do not believe other people's compliments

If you have low self-esteem, people's comments about your strengths ring false. It is worth noting that most self-esteem issues come from childhood and family relationships, a factor that will be discussed later in the chapter on managing relationships.

- You assume the worst too fast

Being pessimistic is defined as tending to see the worst aspect of things or believing that the worst will happen. If you notice that you blow others off for the smallest of reasons, it may be a sign that you have some issues to work through. For example, if a date cancels a dinner date but gives a good reason, you may still refuse to go on another date because you think they are not attracted to you. Sometimes when people give up too fast, they have an inferiority complex and may be leaving for the sake of ego.

Other signs include:

- Continually focusing on upsetting thoughts
- Withdrawing from family members, coworkers, and colleagues
- Shutting down because of embarrassment, shame, guilt, and helplessness
- Taking responsibility for the failures and shortcomings of others
- Seeking validation or attention by faking depression, sickness
- Avoiding any competition where efforts may be compared

An inferiority complex not only hurts you but hurts the people around you as well. The good news is that you do not have to live with it.

Risk Factors and Causes of Inferiority Complex

Before providing corrective actions, it is crucial to understand the root of the problem so that it addressed adequately.

Research suggests that the psychological and behavioral characteristics associated with low self-esteem come from the following factors:

- Genetics

Genetic research has found that people inherit variations in the receptor for oxytocin, the hormone responsible for positive emotions. Some variations cause people to feel less optimistic and to have low self-esteem as well as low personal mastery.

- Family environment

Early caregivers have a significant impact on whether your genetic tendencies toward self-doubt are softened or made worse. A child whose parent is highly critical may internalize their words and carry them into adulthood. During early childhood, you are the most impressionable, and if you face constant criticism, there is a high likelihood that you will grow to feel inferior, powerless, and insecure. The great Greek philosopher Aristotle once said, "Give me a child until he is 7, and I will show you the man."

- Society

There are unrealistic standards all over the place, from social media, advertisers, authority figures, and celebrities that could easily reinforce perceptions about yourself and cause self-doubt. Society is always bombarding you with messages on how to behave, what you should own by a specific age, the size of body that is ideal, the color of hair you should have, and the type of items like cars that is ideal. The messaging is sometimes subliminal. Without realizing it, you could internalize those messages, and they become an internal judge. You start to feel diminished to the point where you deem yourself unworthy.

A general characteristic across all types of people with low self-esteem is that they compare themselves with other people in unhealthy ways. In a world where you will constantly be told to buy things because of their value while you are force-fed a diet of perfection, it is easy for the inferiority complex to become worse. It is often said that it is what is on the inside that matters most. Still, society is more centered around celebrating someone's fame, wealth, car, or bodyweight superficially.

What makes it worse sometimes is that society seems to say one thing and do another, and so when you find yourself feeling less than because you have less, you give in to shame rather than working to better yourself. Shame only compounds the problem.

Part of adopting a positive mindset is knowing when to reject the lie. It is about self-objectivity in considering your shortcomings and working for their improvement. It is not using those shortcomings as a way to define oneself as Caroline in the original example did. It is not about despising oneself. It's about learning self-love, supporting, and encouraging yourself.

What then do you do with your inferiority complex?

Dealing with an inferiority complex

1. Face the emotional memories

Often, if you have an inferiority complex, you have many unhappy feelings that will fuel your thoughts. With this step, examine your thoughts. You can practice journaling with prompts to help you to widen your perspective and to challenge your thoughts. Sometimes you make a conclusion based on one emotionally charged event that is not true across all similar situations. For example, a heartbroken girl may conclude that all men are players when, in fact, every situation is different, and the next guy she meets may very well be the man of her dreams. Journaling will help you to unpack situations and gain perspective on them.

If your feelings are strong, it is advisable to face them head-on. Once you do, your thoughts will naturally become more moderate and manageable.

As an exercise, hone in on the feeling you encounter most that you do not want to have anymore. Close your eyes and access it. If it produces any specific memory where the feeling was shared, that is a memory you need to process.

Also note, it may be challenging to do this exercise the first few times, but once you push through, the impact of the feeling lessens, and the memories keep getting less painful. You can do this exercise with a loved one you trust, but be sure to let them in on what you are doing before you start.

- Be yourself

In the famous words of Oscar Wilde, 'Be yourself, everyone else is already taken' (1890). The best thing you can do in life is to accept who you are and try to be the best version of yourself possible.

The moment that you stop caring what others think about you will become the moment that you're free. One of the things that cripple people is wanting to be like and live like someone else. To do that is to leave behind what makes you unique. You cannot impersonate a person and be true to yourself. It will not make you happy to replicate someone else's life. This is not to say that you cannot learn from other people or have role models.

However, having other people inspire you means that you assimilate some traits they have into yourself. It does not mean that you want the exact life they have. The inferiority complex will thrive when you try to be someone you are not.

- Be specific

Sometimes all you need is to acknowledge whatever it is that makes you feel inferior. What are you inferior about?

Emotional thinking often blows things out of

proportion. Being specific helps you to identify how your thinking is inconsistent with logic. Ask yourself questions that would help to clarify your feelings. For example, of all the people in the world, which ones make you feel inferior? Why?

You may find that you are intimidated by rich people, academic people, good-looking people, or accomplished people. From there, keep zooming in and figure out whether you are being too selective with the people you choose to compare yourself to.

- Dare to live differently

"The only dare you ever want to take is the dare to be all that you can be." – Catherine Pulsifer

Most people are prisoners to the opinions of

others. People are too scared to be themselves. Life is not as restrictive as it was in the past when the only choices a person had were those presented in their village or town. Now, thanks to technology, the options for careers have changed. People are working remotely for employers they have never met. You can wear your hair long or short, and you would be called trendy instead of an outcast. Even what is considered proper official dressing has changed. Many traditional norms have been cast aside. You now have more freedoms than ever before.

The question to ask yourself here is, what do you want to do? Do not worry that it sounds out of the box, and do not tie yourself to what you think you are supposed to do.

- Get rid of the utopian assumptions

Most of the time, when you are feeling inferior, you have all-or-nothing thinking. Utopianism is about regret and a fanciful reality. It's the **'if only...'** thoughts that continuously run through our minds. Many people make the mistake of thinking that they would be happier **if only** they were more attractive, or earned more, or had more things going for them.

Life does not work that way. It is possible that you could be more confident by losing 20 pounds. However, what makes people feel inferior is often more deeply rooted, and achieving the goal may not meet the need. It could leave you wanting more. The goal is to learn to be content and grateful as a human being.

Everyone has deep needs. We long to be loved, to connect, to be useful, and to grow. These needs have to be met to live a life that is fulfilling.

Summary

This chapter zoomed in on inferiority complex and how it stands in the way of a positive mindset. You learned what low self-esteem looks like, how it presents itself, the risk factors, and the causes, and you were equipped to deal with it.

When an inferiority complex rears its ugly head:

- Be specific with your emotions to clarify them
- Eliminate the utopian assumptions
- Face the emotional memories

- Be yourself and
- Dare to live differently!

Chapter 4: Managing Your Emotions

What Are Emotions?

It may sound like a simple question, but it is essential to define what 'emotions' mean in this chapter to understand how it applies to your life and the attitude with which you confront situations.

Different types of those emotions rule your day. You make decisions based on whether you are sad, bored, happy, angry, or frustrated. You choose hobbies and activities based on how they make you feel. It makes sense that you would want to understand them as they can influence how you live life.

According to psychologist Don Hockenbury, emotion is a complicated psychological state that involves three distinct components: a subjective experience, a physiological response, and a behavioral or expressive response (1997).

In 1972, a psychologist suggested six basic emotions to be universal, including surprise, disgust, fear, sadness, anger, and happiness (Eckman, 1972). In 1999, the list was expanded to include satisfaction, excitement, embarrassment, pride, shame, contempt, and amusement.

Scientists have agreed on the major elements of emotions:

- The subjective experience

Experts believe that, universally, people experience some basic emotions, but the experience can be subjective. All anger, for example, is not the same. It can range from blinding rage to mild annoyance. Since emotions are multi-dimensional, they are subjective.

Additionally, you may not experience pure forms of every emotion. You may have mixed emotions over a new job – you could feel both nervous and excited.

- The physiological response

There is a reason poets describe being in love beginning with butterflies in the stomach. You may have experienced a faster heart rate when you were afraid or a stomach lurch from anxiety. Whatever your situation, you notice that emotions cause a physiological reaction.

Many of the responses, like a racing heartbeat or sweaty palms, are regulated by the sympathetic nervous system, a part of the autonomic nervous system that deals with involuntary body responses like digestion and blood flow. It is in charge of flight or fight.

- The behavioral response

Consciously or not, you spend plenty of time looking at and assigning meaning to other people's behaviors and facial expressions. This makes the last component. The ability to interpret what someone means or how they are feeling based on their body language (facial expressions, gestures, and so forth) is tied to emotional intelligence.

Research suggests that some expressions are universal, like a smile when someone is happy, but there are cultural and social norms that affect how emotions are interpreted and expressed. In Japan, for example, people mask displays of disgust or fear in the presence of an authority figure.

Emotions versus moods

In daily communication, people use 'moods' and

'emotions' interchangeably, but according to psychologists, there are some distinctions.

An emotion is short-lived and intense. It is likely to have an identifiable cause. For instance, after a disagreement over politics, you may feel angry for a while.

On the other hand, a mood is mild but lasts longer. It is often difficult to pinpoint the cause of the mood. For example, you could feel gloomy for some days without a good reason.

Here are some short descriptions of three key emotions that you may want to learn to manage in the context of this book:

- Sadness

Sadness can be defined as a transient state

characterized by grief, disinterest, disappointment, hopelessness, and a dampened mood. It is a normal emotion to experience from time to time, but sometimes people can experience it for prolonged periods like when you are depressed. It is expressed through crying, quietness, lethargy, and withdrawing from others. It could lead you to engage in coping mechanisms like avoidance and ruminating on negative thoughts, both of which stand in the way of being positive.

- Fear

Fear can play a significant role in survival. When in danger, your muscles tense, respiration and heart rate increase, and your mind is more alert to prime the body to respond appropriately. This response helps deal with threats, but if left unchecked, it can spiral out of control. Some people experience intense fear out of perceived threat or potential danger, and this is called anxiety.

- Anger

Anger can be especially powerful, characterized by feelings of agitation, hostility, frustration, and antagonism toward other people. Uncontrolled anger can cause aggressive behaviors like kicking, hitting, and hurling objects.

All emotions can have physical and mental consequences if unchecked, but this book will focus on the effects of the three and their combined emotions like embarrassment, contempt, guilt, and shame.

Why Should You Manage Emotions?

Here is an unpopular opinion: Most of the problems you have with productivity have very little to do with ideas, techniques, or tools.

Think about it, there is now, more than ever, more access to proper techniques and tools to be productive, and yet people struggle just as much.

Have you installed task management apps that have not helped with procrastination? Is it unlikely that you have emails in your inbox after you last checked two minutes ago, but you still check? Have you read books about productivity and organization, but you still waste time on unimportant things, ignoring the important tasks? What about notebooks and planners – how many do you have and how effective are they?

Are you starting to get the point?

The problem may be a bit complicated when you dig into each individual situation, but most times, it boils down to poor emotion management. Emotion management is about your reaction to strong emotions. How do you deal with sudden anxiety? What is your go-to for dealing with anger? What pops into your mind when you are criticized or ashamed?

If these questions appear difficult, it may be because you have some areas to improve when it comes to managing emotions. Think about it; from a young age, you learn how to be physically fit, how to manage finances, time management, but rarely do you learn how to manage emotions.

What you end up learning comes from emulating adults unconsciously. In other words, if your parent hit the wall when mad, you may have learned that it is okay to get physical when angry.

It is okay if your emotion management skills are unrefined, but you cannot afford to ignore working on them.

Across domains like parenting, healthcare, and investing, difficult emotions will be sure to show up. Your success in life in any area will depend on how successfully you can manage the scary emotions. It also helps with personal productivity.

As an example of how poor emotion

management can get in the way of your productivity, think about procrastination. Everyone struggles with procrastination every once in a while, but it is not obvious why this happens. Imagine a day when you are trying to get a task done. You try the first time, and then the internet goes down, or you are interrupted by a phone call. You try again and find it not going as you hoped. You open your email. Before long, you decide that tomorrow is as good a day to do it as any.

Without realizing it, something psychological happened behind your procrastination. The first mistake was trying to do the task without remembering your tendencies to procrastinate, and then your mind duped you again. There are a few things to pick from this example that count as reasons to learn to manage emotions:

- Mindlessness is the enemy – If you are not vigilant when doing hard things, your emotions rule. You stand a better chance of managing the emotions when you go into the task with self-awareness.
- Your mind will resist any difficult task – This does not mean that there is a problem. It is an evolutionary heritage that the brain is always trying to save energy, so when negative self-talk begins to rear its head, you have to be aware.

Managing Emotions

To navigate through the emotional war, you have to make some major distinctions:

1. Emotions are not as easy to control – you are not a switch

Your emotions will come whether you want them or not. Once you have this settled in your mind, you can stop waiting for the emotions you do not want to go. Imagining that you can banish your emotions is not helpful and will work against you. Emotions are part of being a human being. Besides, the more you work to live according to the things you value and your commitments, the more your emotions will arise to challenge you.

2. Emotions are not negative or positive.

It is a common distinction – happiness is positive, sadness is negative, and so on. It is understandable too. The human brain cannot help but categorize things as negative or positive. It is very alert to threats.

According to modern evolutionary theory, primal emotions like fear are associated with the ancient brain parts and are suspected of having evolved among the pre-mammal ancestors. At the time, you needed to respond fast to stimuli to survive (Darwin, 1859).

Now, thanks to technology and many changes that have happened over time, life is less threatening, and you no longer need to rely on emotions in the sense of survival. Managing emotions will require you to recognize that sometimes, you will experience emotions that are not equal to the problem, and that is just alright. Rather than thinking of them as negative or positive, think of them as messengers and throw away the classifications.

3. You are not your emotions.

By their nature, emotions are intense. In the throes of an emotion like anger, you can think of yourself as an angry person. However, remind yourself that you are a human with commitments and values who happens to have some emotions triggered by certain situations. If this is your first time interacting with this idea, it may seem like it has no implications on real life, but that is not true. When you become fused to your emotions, they are in control. The alternative is observing your emotions without letting them determine how you behave.

4. You always have a choice.

A feeling or a thought on its own does not stand in the way of you acting. It is easy to make the jump from 'I am scared' to 'I can't speak', but that is the mind working at a very primal level to protect you from a perceived threat. The more authentic and accurate way is to say, 'I am scared and deciding not to speak.' The ability to observe your emotions – even the powerful ones – allows you to create space to reference your values and commitments. You do not get to choose the feelings you have, but you can choose how you respond to them. The heart of this is responsibility – which is the closest thing to a power you will ever have.

With these four distinctions forming the basis of your choices, how then can you improve your emotion management skills and get more productive?

For starters, you are bound to meet many opinions about managing emotions, and people will always have differences as a result of history, personality, struggles, culture, and so forth. Still, there are some general principles that can help you with your circumstance.

- Observe self-talk

Cognition will always go before emotion. In actuality, this looks like your productivity being derailed by negative emotion that comes as a result of subtle and powerful self-talk happening behind the scenes. Learning to observe your self-talk can help you to change your habits of thinking that you do not want and is vital in managing emotion effectively.

- Improve your vocabulary

Most people have poor emotional awareness because their vocabulary and framework for considering their emotional states is not sophisticated enough. By refining and expanding your emotional vocabulary, you can improve your self-awareness and hence your ability to manage and tolerate difficult emotions.

- Be mindful

The term mindfulness has been used a lot recently, and it could easily become cliché. However, rightly practiced and considered, it can prove vital to building your emotion management skills and improving your mental health in general. It is simply the art of keeping your attention on something you value and regulating it so that your feelings do not take hold.

- Work with a coach

There was a time you could not talk about seeing a therapist or a life coach with a straight face. There was a stigma associated with seeking help, and people assumed the worst. Nowadays, thanks to an increase in awareness, people are more open to the idea of finding help. It is much easier to find a guiding hand for a situation you find difficult. Bear in mind that an outside eye can see something that you are missing and help you in the right direction.

How Does That Connect with a Positive Outlook?

What is the use of emotional management in the context of having a positive mindset? One of the major roadblocks to being positive, as was mentioned in an earlier chapter, is emotional thinking. Being able to manage your emotions gets rid of that specific roadblock. Consider these:

- The perception of emotion

This is the ability to pinpoint emotional messages in someone's tone of voice, facial expressions, and even artistic works. People who have emotional perception of their own emotions and those of others have many advantages in social situations, and they will likely be more empathetic as they can see things from a perspective different from their own.

- Emotions to help thinking

Based on the understanding that you are not your emotions, you can rely on them to understand what you should do in a given situation. For example, if you find that you are beginning to get resentful about a situation, instead of concluding that you are generally a disagreeable person, you can alternatively unpack the situation and find out the ways that you need to grow up and how you need to speak up for yourself.

As a rule, when you are happy, you think positively, and when you are sad, you tend to have negative thoughts. When emotions are correctly used, you will first acknowledge them. From there, you ask yourself questions in a journal or when talking with a friend you trust, to help you understand the problem and to make decisions that make your life better.

- Understanding emotions

It is one thing to notice that you are feeling annoyed. However, you need to be able to know the message the emotion carries. Where is it coming from? Where can it lead you to? As an example, irritation can lead to anger or feelings of insecurity, which could cause unpredictable outbursts. Emotionally intelligent people can label their emotions appropriately and understand even complicated emotional states.

Emotional management is not getting rid of troubling emotions. It is about learning to control them. Have you ever found that when you are upset, you think that there is nothing to do? Or perhaps you try to escape to something else. Whatever the case, successful emotional management is being able to deal with whatever comes at you in a healthy and appropriate manner.

Limiting beliefs

"We all have unlimited potential — but often, our results don't reflect that. Why? Because our unconscious beliefs cripple our results. The only thing that's keeping you from getting what you want is the story you keep telling yourself."
– Tony Robbins, 1991

Sometimes, what is standing in the way of positive thinking is a limiting belief. Think back to your earliest memories as a child – do you remember being fearless? To what places did curiosity take you?

Like most people, you may notice that as you grew older, you were introduced to a long list of rules about the things you are supposed to say, how you should behave, and who you should be. Unchecked, these rules can become limiting beliefs instead of guides to help you do better in life.

To clarify, this is not a campaign to throw all the rules into the wind. Some rules exist for your benefit. However, this section is for someone who feels that they are boxed in when it comes to something they would like to do.

So what exactly is a limiting belief?

In short, a limiting belief is a mindset or belief that we make about ourselves that limits the way you think and live. It could be about you, the people you interact with, or even the world and the manner in which things run.

Here is a list of the most common limiting

beliefs we tell ourselves:

- "I don't have the time."
- "It's too expensive."
- "I don't have the willpower."
- "I don't understand."
- "All the good ones are already taken."
- "I am scared of rejection."
- "I'll never find true love."
- "I don't have what it takes to succeed."
- "I don't have the talent."
- "I could never do that."
- "Successful people are just lucky."
- "Rich people are greedy."
- "I'm not good with money."
- "I'll never make enough money."
- "I can't afford that."
- "I'll never be able to retire."
- "Things will never change."

Limiting beliefs have many boundless negative effects on our lives. It could keep you from making choices that are good for you, taking advantage of new opportunities, and achieving your dreams. Ultimately, the belief keeps you stuck in a frame of mind that hinders you from living your life the way you desire.

Here are a few causes of limiting beliefs. Which one do you resonate with?

- Fear of Failure

The fear of failure is the most common fear holding us back from success. The truth is, there is no such thing as failure; there are only results. Fear destroys our mindset and immobilizes us from taking action.

- Family beliefs

Your upbringing shapes the way you think the world should look. It forms the career paths you take, the way you engage with others, and your behaviors. It is easy to develop limiting beliefs based on what you learned growing up. For example, if parents reinforce a belief that you should never challenge authority, you could become someone who does not speak up for themselves. You may believe that unfair treatment from an authority figure should be accepted. You may even be unable to recognize it.

- Education

Education plays a vital role in the limiting beliefs people adopt. Whether you are learning from friends, family, or teachers, they all impact what you accept as truth. This is because they are constantly sharing ideas, beliefs, and information on the way the world works. When you are learning from people you respect, you are more inclined to conclude whatever they tell you to be true.

- Past Experiences

When you have experiences in life, or when you make certain choices, it is common to draw conclusions based on a previous outcome. For instance, if you love someone and you get heartbroken, you could conclude that love always ends in pain. Negative experiences tend to have a shaping ability on the things you believe. It is vital to remember that your conclusions are valid only for a short time.

Identifying limiting beliefs

If limiting beliefs were easy to identify, everyone would do it, and they would be living the kind of life they want to. To recognize your limiting beliefs, you have to be willing to look within yourself and notice without judgment things that you may not even want to face. It is advisable to take a pen and paper and give yourself some time at a place you feel comfortable.

Once you have the pen and paper, do the following:

1. Identify your surface beliefs

Begin by writing down the things that you believe in general. What is it that you feel strongly about? Write also the things that influence your life every day. You can group the beliefs into different categories like relationships, career, finances, health, and family. After the exercise, examine the ones that help you to grow. Anything else may be a limiting belief.

2. Assess how you behave

Another way to know your limiting beliefs is to examine the way you behave. Consider the times you have acted in toxic or harmful ways. Why did you do that? If you look keenly at your negative behaviors, you may find that the root cause driving your actions is a limiting belief. For example, if you have a hard time telling someone when they offend you, you may believe that conflict is bad. In turn, this could be keeping you from a truly intimate relationship.

3. Note the areas you feel challenged

If you have noticed some challenges that recur in different areas of your life, this could be because you have a limiting belief. Maybe you are unable to find a well-paid job. Or perhaps, you are unlucky in love. The challenges may be because you have adopted some untruths as truth. As you consider every challenge, write it down and note the beliefs associated with the challenge.

Overcoming limiting beliefs

Now that you have identified the beliefs that are limiting your growth, it is crucial to understand that you have the power to change. The process will not be easy, but once you commit to improvement, you will see results. To get you started, here are some tips:

- Take action toward the empowering belief

Little action equals mediocre results. The more resolved beliefs we have about achieving something, the more potential we have to accomplish it. Rather than believing, "I don't have the willpower." Start believing, "I must get it done." And take massive action towards that goal.

- Declutter

Most people are not aware that their environment can affect the things they believe. Having a spacious and well-organized environment can encourage positive thinking and improve your mental space. A tidy environment will give you space to think and gain clarity.

To do this, remove the clutter that you have accumulated over time. You can even redesign the flow and space in your home as an exercise in rearranging your psyche. The basic premise is keeping the flow of energy in your home by arranging things in a specific way.

As you do this, get rid of anything you do not like. You will notice that the exercise will influence your mind and help you to keep your thoughts on constructive things.

- Try Minimalism

Minimalism can help you to identify any false beliefs and to get rid of them. The fundamentals of the practice are honesty, detaching from material possessions, and clarity. For instance, if you are continually adding new clothing to your wardrobe, it could be that the limiting belief concerns your physical appearance. You could believe that you are not attractive if you do not have on the latest fashion. Minimalism is about resisting peer pressure and your mindset. It will help you to embrace a more meaningful lifestyle.

- Explore

Limiting beliefs and closed-mindedness are closely related. To open your mind, let curiosity be your guide. When you give in to it, you will likely explore the world around you and get out of your comfort zone. Curiosity will create learning opportunities for you. You can start by talking with people whose backgrounds differ from yours. Traveling also helps to develop an open mind.

The world is full of beliefs and different people. This will not change. You have to find a way to adopt beliefs that support the way of life you dream of. Any idea that keeps you from that life is one to eliminate.

Conditioning empowering beliefs

Once you are ready to commit to a new empowering belief, you must condition this new belief into your subconscious. Here are some ways you can do this:

- Practice visualization

Visualization has been used for ages by successful people to picture their desired outcomes. It gives you what appears to the onlooker like superpowers, helping you to create your dream life by accomplishing one task or goal at a time. Elite athletes use visualization to focus on their goals. It activates the subconscious, which generates creative ideas to achieve that goal. It programs the brain to recognize and see resources needed in the service of the goal, it activates the law of attraction, and it helps to build your internal motivation to do what you need to do to achieve your dreams.

Visualization is simple - Sit in a comfortable place and close your eyes. Imagine in as much detail as you can. Imagine looking out through your eyes when you have reached the ideal. Do this a few minutes every day. The best time is after you wake up and right before going to bed. Follow the following steps:

a. Imagine sitting in a theater. Dim the lights and have the movie start. The movie is of your life and the changes that happen when you have embraced the new belief. Picture as many details as you can, including what you are wearing, your body movements, and the expressions on your face. Recreate in your body the feelings you would associate with the activity.

b. Leave your chair and move to the screen. Enter into the movie and experience it again inside of yourself. This is referred to as the 'embodied image' instead of the 'distant image.' It will deepen your experience.

c. Walk back out of the screen and return to your seat. Grab the screen and shrink it to the size of a cracker. Put the tiny screen into your mouth and swallow. Imagine each piece like a hologram containing the picture of the successful you. Think of the screens moving through your bloodstream into every cell in your body.

- Anchoring

An anchor holds your attention to help you focus on the desirable belief you want to hold instead of drifting away. In the process of anchoring, you associate an internal response with a trigger outside so that the belief can be re-accessed quickly. A psychological anchor will act as a reference point to stabilize the mental state you want.

There are factors that will contribute to the power of an anchor, including the intensity and richness of the experience, its emotional level, and the continuous reinforcement of the anchor. The idea is simple; when two events happen close together enough times, they become associated with each other. Use the following steps:

> a. Think of the belief you want to adopt. Think back to a time when you embodied it, like when you

won a prize or received some good news or even your first kiss.

b. Tell the story of what happened in your head and the events that lead to that moment. Describe them as vividly as you can until you remember the feeling.

c. Hold your middle and left index fingers in your right hand and squeeze gently. As you squeeze another time, make the picture in your head last longer.

d. Describe the feeling again and your thoughts at the time while squeezing the fingers the same way.

You can repeat this process for as many times as you like until the action triggers the thoughts and feelings immediately. You can make the action anything you want.

- Emotional Freedom Technique (EFT)

EFT can help you when you are in emotional distress because of a limiting belief. The technique is founded on research that found that a disruption in energy causes pain and negative emotions. The technique is about balancing your energy system.

There are energy spots in the body that you can tap to restore its energy and relieve the symptoms of a negative experience. You can use the following steps to address different issues:

   a. Find the issue -This technique will only be effective if you know what belief you want to address. It will be your focal point as you tap. Focus on only one belief at a time.

b. Test its initial intensity – After finding the problem, benchmark its intensity and rate anywhere between 0 and 10. 10 is the most difficult. The scale is an assessment of the discomfort you feel from the main issue. A benchmark helps to monitor progress.

c. The set up – Establish a phrase explaining the belief you want to change. You want to focus on acknowledging the issue and self-acceptance. A set up could sound like: 'Even if I have (this problem), I completely accept myself.' You can change the phrase to fit your issue.

d. The tapping sequence – EFT tapping sequence addresses nine meridian points. There are 12 major points mirroring each side of the body and corresponding to an organ. Still, EFT focuses on the small intestine meridian (karate chop), the governing vessel (top of the head), bladder meridian (eyebrow), gallbladder meridian (side of the eye), stomach meridian (under the eye), governing vessel (under the nose), the central vessel (chin), kidney (beginning of the collarbone), and spleen meridian (under the arm). Start by tapping the karate chop as you recite your set-up phrase thrice. Tap the rest of the points in the order they are listed. Finish the sequence at the top of the head point. Be sure to keep you focus on the problem area as you recite the setup phrase and repeat the sequence up to three times.

e. Testing the intensity – After the sequence, use the scale of 0 to 10 and compare the intensity levels. Repeat until you reach an intensity level of zero.

- Emulating people who actively live the empowering belief

You can be the best person at something in the world, but if you do not present yourself that way, you will not feel confident. One way to overcome a limiting belief and translate that feeling of inner confidence is to find someone to emulate.

Do you know someone who lives out the empowering belief? That's an excellent start. Now assume that you are an understudy and watch what they do, their mannerisms, what they say, and how they present themselves to people. Practice doing the same things. As a rule of thumb, find someone who does not intimidate you.

When you emulate someone, you set yourself free from your identity. It does not matter how unconfident, introverted, or clumsy you feel. If you walk into a room and assume the belief you want, you will begin to feel it. Over time, it will come naturally to you and carry you through other situations.

<u>Summary</u>

Emotions are a big part of having a positive mindset. They inform the decisions you make. You can use them as a friend, or you can leave them, and they would work against you. The basis of emotional management is understanding that:

- You are not your emotions
- Emotions are neither positive nor negative; acknowledging them without labels is best
- You always have a choice when it comes to responding

- You cannot switch off emotions or switch them on – you have to learn to negotiate with yourself

With these factors as the basis for your emotion management, you can work to counter mindlessness and adopt the suggested methods including:

- Watching your self-talk
- Improving your vocabulary
- Being mindful
- Enlisting the help of a coach if you need it.

This chapter also looks into limiting beliefs and helps you to identify and overcome them using neurolinguistic programming techniques like anchoring, EFT, and visualization.

Develop a Positive Mindset and Attract the Life of Your Dreams

Chapter 5: Managing Your Relationships

People define relationships differently, but most agree that for a relationship to be healthy, there has to be some components like honesty, openness, and safe communication. For any kind of relationship, you have to be sure you understand each other's expectations and needs so that you are on the same page. You cannot be on the same page if you do not talk to each other.

As a rule of thumb, if something is bothering you in a relationship, you have to be willing to talk about it rather than keep it in. Each person in the relationship bears the responsibility to make themselves a safe place for the other. One way to do this is to respect the feelings and wishes of the other person. You want to let them know that you are putting an effort to think about their ideas as you make choices.

Compromise is also an essential feature of relationships. Even healthy relationships have disagreements, but you have to figure out a way to solve conflicts rationally and fairly when they happen.

A healthy relationship is not based on control and power; it is based on respect and equality.

It is important to remember that you cannot have relationships if you are unwilling to be who you truly are in front of your friends or partner. Yet, there is a measure of wisdom in controlling who you let into your personal space. They could influence the way you think and get in the way or support whatever dreams and ambitions you may have.

Good Relationships? Why?

Human beings are, by nature, social beings – you crave positive interactions and friendships the way you crave water and food. It makes sense that the better your relationships, the more productive, happy, and positive you will be.

Good relationships at work, for example, make the environment more enjoyable. People will be more likely to comply if there are any changes to implement if they have good relationships. It also helps with creativity and innovation.

Good relationships anywhere will give you freedom. Rather than spend your energy and time overcoming the problems of negative relationships, you can focus on the opportunities that come your way. They help to develop careers. Imagine a boss who does not trust you – how likely are they to promote you when it is time?

It is often said that the 'ship' in the term relationship is a reference to the fact that the relationship either sinks or floats. While that is not entirely true, it is useful to think about the relationships in that perspective and consider which ones are worth keeping.

What Makes a Good Relationship?

Here are the keys to a healthy relationship:

- Trust – This forms the basis of every relationship. When you trust a colleague, teammate, or friend, you develop a powerful bond that will help with effective communication. You tell them your thoughts openly, your actions are easy to understand, and people do not have to waste their time 'watching their back' with you.
- Mutual respect – when you respect someone, you value their ideas and input as they do yours. You work together to

come up with solutions based on your collective creativity, insight, and wisdom.

- Mindfulness – This is taking responsibility for your actions and words. Mindful people are careful about what they say. They will not let their negative emotions affect their friends.
- Embracing diversity – Good relationships not only accept diversity in people, but they also embrace diverse opinions and even welcome them. For example, when your colleagues and friends offer a view that is different from yours, you consider what they say and factor their insights into your decision.
- Open communication – People are always communicating through messages, emails, and face to face. The more effectively you communicate, the

richer the relationships will be. Every good relationship depends on honest and open communication.

Relationships at Work

It makes sense to try and maintain good working relationships with all people, but some relationships deserve more attention.

For instance, you will benefit from a good relationship with major stakeholders in your company, as those are people who have a say in your failure or success. Forming a bond with them helps you to make sure your career and projects are on track.

Tips for building good work relationships

You spend a lot of your life at work, so it makes

sense that you would want to build better relationships. You do not want the environment you go to every day to be what stands in the way of a positive outlook in life.

- Develop people skills

Good relationships begin with well-developed people skills. How are your soft skills? How well do you communicate, collaborate, and handle conflict?

- Know your relationship needs

What is it that you need from others? What do they need from you? Understanding needs can be crucial to having better relationships.

- Schedule time to make better relationships

Devote a chunk of your day, even if it is simply 20 minutes spread throughout the day, toward building relationships. You could check up on someone at lunchtime, reply to their LinkedIn or Twitter, or ask someone to a cup of coffee. The little interactions create the basis for a good relationship.

- Build your emotional intelligence

If you are going to have good relationships, you need to spend some time developing how well you recognize your own emotions and understanding the message they portray. The more you improve your emotional intelligence, the better you will be able to understand the needs and emotions of others.

- Say "Thank You"

When someone helps you, be keen to show appreciation. Everyone from your office cleaner to your boss wants to be appreciated for what they do. Compliment people genuinely, and that will open the doors to closer relationships.

- Manage your boundaries

Be sure to manage and set boundaries appropriately. Boundaries help you to interact with people in a way that you feel respected. They help you to have an impact without feeling taken advantage of. If you notice that a colleague or a friend has a monopoly on your time, you may need to assert your boundaries so that you can have time to work and time for social interactions.

- Do not gossip

Office politics can kill relationships at work. If you have a conflict with someone within your group, address it with them. If you gossip about the situation, you will only make it worse and create animosity and mistrust.

- Listen actively

When talking to colleagues and customers, practice active listening. People respond well when others genuinely hear what they have to say. Listen more than you speak, and you will be someone that people can trust.

Ten Tips to Keep Any Relationship Healthy

Other than your work relationships, you have to care for your relationship with your significant other, friends outside of work, and family members. It is easy to make things more complicated than they should be, so follow the following basic rules to begin moving in the right direction:

1. Good relationships take work

Remember that movie when the girl met a boy and they were married in 90 minutes? Well, that is only true in movies. Good relationships do not happen in a vacuum. The parties involved have to risk sharing what is happening in their heads and hearts.

2. You can only change yourself; you cannot change anyone else

If you love a person and think that they will change the way they behave to get rid of things you are uncomfortable with, you need to rethink your strategy. If you want anything to change, discuss with your partner so that they know what you need, but remember that you can only change yourself.

3. All arguments come from pain or fear

When you are upset or hurt, find out what is happening in the other person's mind instead of getting angry with them. You will find that people are not usually upset for the reasons you think.

4. Understand gender differences

Men may not be from Mars and women from Venus, but the differences between the genders are inevitable and part of biology. You can either learn to celebrate and understand them or make other people's lives miserable, trying to mold them into your own image.

5. Honor each other every day

There is a popular saying that every day is a second chance. Take as many opportunities as you need to make your relationship deeper and gratifying. Feeling cherished and respected by someone you love makes life easier.

6. Anger wastes time

Anger kills relationships because it is self-absorbed and blinding. When you are annoyed with someone, allow yourself time to keep calm, and then gently discuss what is happening in your mind.

7. Regular tune-ups are a necessity

It is okay to read a book on relationships, even when everything is going well. You may pick up some ideas that could strengthen the connection you have.

8. Find ways to stay close

This is more important in romantic relationships but cuts across every type of relationship. Find creative ways to devote more time together.

9. Take responsibility for your happiness

No person can give you happiness. It is something you have to give yourself. If you start to feel that someone else is the reason you are unhappy, look inside and identify what you are missing.

10. Give what you would like to get

People's needs are ever-changing. If you want to be understood, try to be understanding. If you want to feel love, try giving it more. This is a simple rule, but it works. You want to be proactive in your relationships.

Difficult Relationships

You want all your relationships to go well, but occasionally, you will have to collaborate with people you would rather not work with or people you cannot relate to. For the sake of work, for example, you have to keep the relationship professional.

When this is the case, you want to make an effort to know that person. They likely know you are not on good terms, so you may want to make the first move to work on the relationship. As a rule of thumb, make sure that your conversation is genuine. Try not to be so guarded that it is impossible to get close. Ask about their interests, background, and successes in the past. Remember not to focus on your differences, but try to find the things you have in common.

Keep in mind that not all relationships will be great, but they could at least be workable.

When you have done everything you can, and it still does not work, it may be time to end the relationship.

Tips for Ending a Bad Relationship

Moving on is not always easy. You may have difficulties convincing yourself that that is the right thing to do.

As a way of assurance, if a relationship makes you more miserable than happy and your heart is not right, you do not have to hold on to the relationship. It may not mean that you are wrong or that they are, just that you are not right for each other. If you feel stuck, the following are research-based psychological strategies to help you make that difficult decision:

- Separate love and addiction

Neurochemically speaking, love and addiction are similar. Studies show that when partners are intensely in love and they see images of their beloved, the brain region that is activated is the same region that gets activated in drug addicts when they crave a fix. However, even though love has some qualities that look like addiction, healthy love should also have other attributes like trust, commitment, and respect. These are qualities that will keep the relationship strong even when the passion and excitement are not at the top.

Addictive love is focused on getting to the 'highs' whatever the cost. The people involved have unpredictable behaviors – like not calling when they promise to. They will likely keep you hooked because their inconsistent affection always leaves you wanting more.

While trying to get out of any relationship that feels more like an addiction than a loving bond, you will need to reframe your emotions and thoughts about the person. This may require you to get some healthy distance – you can go for a while without calling until the longing reduces. When you are overwhelmed, acknowledge the feeling but do not act on it.

- Take a break

Your family and friends can be divided into two categories:

I. The ones who make you feel good, who always reassure you, and with whom you are confident that everything will work.
II. The ones who continuously drain your energy with subtle and blatant implications that you are weak, silly, or pathetic.

If you find yourself drawn to both, you want comfort, but you also need the motivation to change. One way to achieve this without berating or deluding yourself is to practice self-compassion. Self-compassion involves reassuring yourself that you are not a horrible person and that it is understandable to love someone you would prefer not to. Many people get into this kind of situation. Self-compassion is about caring for yourself and seeking your best interests. It involves you re-parenting yourself, which may mean leaving a relationship that keeps hurting you.

- Create a plan

Research has proven that you are more likely to make lasting changes when you create specific goals rather than 'if/then' plans. When you have a specific plan, you can break it down into simple steps that you can do every day. That way, you do not have to wonder about the way forward, and you are more gracious when relating to others.

It is possible that when leaving a relationship, you have many if/then connections. On examination, you will find that they do not work in your favor. An example is thinking: "If I am lonely and missing my partner, I will call them and invite them over." Instead, take up a habit that will make you a better person in the long run, like listening to empowering messages or reading. The more you make different choices, the more you get rid of the 'if' stimulus and the automatic links attached. You will make it easier to resist the old patterns.

- Fight cognitive dissonance

Your mind has sneaky ways of justifying your

actions so that you do not feel like you made a mistake or did a stupid thing. This is called cognitive dissonance. It is the reason you find yourself loyal to a group that caused you suffering. It is also why bad relationships are difficult to break free from, especially when you have been in the relationship for an extended period.

Unless things in the relationship went awry suddenly, ending a relationship often means reconciling with the fact that you did not end it when you could have, and that was a mistake you made. If you are unable to reconcile with this, you might keep rationalizing your commitment to the relationship to justify the past decision to stay in it. It helps to be aware of the tricks of the mind to avoid the trap.

- Own your decision

Ending a relationship can be a painful and prolonged struggle that is difficult to do alone. You may need to get the support of someone else to help you keep the course and to fill your life with positive and healthy activities. Ultimately though, the choice to end it has to be yours. Succumbing to outside pressure will not last you long. When other things fail, it helps to ask yourself what you really want and accept the answer.

Summary

In this chapter, you have learned how integral relationships are to your mindset. If you are constantly interacting with people who put you on the defense or people who are toxic for you, it will be harder to stay positive.

You have learned how to foster healthy relationships by growing your people skills, scheduling time for relationships you care about, establishing and maintaining boundaries, knowing your needs, and seeking to meet them.

Healthy relationships:

- Take work
- Require you to change yourself, not the other person
- Need regular tune-ups
- Need a proper understanding of arguments and where they stem from
- Rely on ways people put in place to stay close
- Require that parties take responsibility for their happiness
- Need reciprocity

- Need healthy ways to deal with anger
- Require honor

Unfortunately, not all relationships you will be in will be healthy or have people working to make them better. When you encounter difficult relationships, you have to be equipped to end them by:

- Separating love and addiction
- Fighting cognitive dissonance
- Taking a break when you need it
- Creating a plan
- Owning your choice to end the relationship

Develop a Positive Mindset and Attract the Life of Your Dreams

Chapter 6: Neuro-Linguistic Programming

Neuro-linguistic programming (NLP) is like a user manual for your brain. The previous chapter concentrated on your external environment. While that is significant to the way you live and think, the ultimate battle has to be won in your brain, and NLP can help with that.

Beginning the 1970s, researchers found out that NLP techniques can be effective in changing the way you experience the world. Since your feelings and thoughts shape your reality, this means that using techniques that alter those thoughts and feelings can change the trajectory of your life.

NLP is about offering practical ways to change the way you think. It changes how you interact with the events in your past and ultimately affects your approach to life. The techniques discussed in this chapter will show you how to control your life by controlling your mind. Where psychotherapy focuses on the 'why', NLP focuses on the 'how' and gives you practical guidelines.

It was co-created by psychotherapists Richard

Bandler and Virginia Satir. Bandler noticed that the conventional techniques used in psychotherapy did not always work. He was concerned with finding different ways to solve problems. NLP was born as a result of techniques that worked well with their patients.

The principle behind NLP is taking control of one's mind. You may not have much control over what is happening around you, but you can control the thoughts you have about it. This stems from an understanding that your thoughts, emotions, and feelings are not things that you have or things that define you; they are choices that you make. You choose to think a particular way. The root causes may be complicated and could range from the comments of people, to beliefs from your teachers, parents, or even events you went through.

NLP will show you how to control your influences and beliefs. Using mind techniques like reframing content can change how you feel and think about events of the past, phobias, and fears from the perspective that while you cannot control what happens, you can control how you handle it.

NLP is inherently connected with the power of belief. If you are convinced that something bad will happen, no matter the evidence to the contrary, your brain will only focus on the negative, and something bad will inevitably happen. On the converse, if you believe that something will make you better, you will often become better – like with medical experiments and the placebo effect.

The bottom line here is that whatever you believe yourself capable of achieving is possible for you. However, you have to challenge your limiting beliefs. Ask questions like – How can I be sure I can do that? When did I first think I cannot? How was that wrong?

The other pillar of NLP is setting goals. There are universally known principles of setting goals, but NLP suggests some additional insights focusing less on dissatisfaction and more on satisfaction.

For instance, your goals must be positive so that you focus on the things you want and not the things you lose in your efforts to get what you want. You are to think about the things you truly want – for example, it is not the purchase of a dream house that drives you, but the hope of living in it. It is easier to stay motivated about a goal that gives you satisfaction.

NLP believes in the power of questions and their ability to help with clarity. According to Bandler, the mind is set up to look for answers to questions actively. If you ask yourself a question like 'why am I feeling so bad?', your mind will come up with many answers, and you will likely feel worse. When using NLP, it is not just about asking questions but asking the right questions like – why do I want to change? What do I need to focus on to improve? What will life look like after I have changed?

NLP uses questions whose natural result is a positive outlook. Here are a few tools used in NLP:

- Moving images

Bring the image of a person who aggravates you to mind. What does the picture look like in your mind? Zoom the image out, change it to black and white, and then imagine the image fading away. How does that make you feel? Now imagine the picture of something that evokes positive feelings in you. Zoom it in and make it brighter and more prominent. As it moves closer to you, how does it make you feel?

The idea of moving images is about allowing this thought process to help you to recognize the effect of events and people and to understand what you feel about them. By playing around with the images, you teach your brain how to focus on the good feelings and to ignore the bad feelings.

- Diminishing the inner voice

Most people will admit to having an inner critical voice in their heads that shows up at the worst of times. It says things like 'that sounds so hard for a person like you,' or 'you are not able to do that.' The next time that critical voice speaks up imagine that it sounds like Tweety Bird or Donald Duck. How do the changes make you feel about the wisdom of that voice? If the voice does not sound real, it will be easier to silence.

- Playing a movie backward

If you just went through a difficult experience and you are having a hard time processing it, imagine if it happened backward. Begin from the point when you realized that it was finally over. Now imagine the incident unfolding backward until you get to a time before it starts. Do this several times until you know how the film unfolds in reverse. Now make it small in your mind - maybe so little that you can only see it on your phone –and play it backward. Eventually, think of a different end to that experience as long as it makes you smile. Do you feel the change in your emotions? The principal technique is that your brain learns another way to think of a memory to change the way you respond to it.

- Brilliance squared

Consider an emotion that you are interested in feeling, like confidence. Imagine that there is a colored square before you and the color of it is the one you associate with the emotion. Now imagine you are standing on the square and it is full of that emotion. How would you stand? What would be the look in your face? What about your posture? Step inside the square and behave like the imaginary you. What feeling spreads through you? Keep repeating until the process comes easy. Now imagine the square before you and enter. What does it feel like? The trick here is to train your mind to make associations of a feeling and an image. When you conjure the image, you will conjure the feeling.

Hopefully, these examples have demonstrated NLP to be a powerful tool based on the power of your mind. Some people may think of them as mind tricks, but relying on these tried techniques teaches you how to control your mind and your responses to it.

Here are five techniques to use on your journey to becoming a more positive person:

Dissociation

Have you ever found yourself in a situation that evokes a bad feeling in you? Perhaps it is an experience that reminded you of a previous experience, or maybe it is something that makes you feel down each time you encounter it. Do you get nervous when a specific person approaches you? – a crush, perhaps? These feelings of nervousness, sadness, or shyness can appear to be unstoppable or automatic, but the NLP technique of dissociation can help you.

Identify the emotion that you feel — is it discomfort, rage, fear, or dislike for the situation? Do you want to get rid of it? Now imagine that you had the ability to float outside your body and see yourself from outside — the idea is to give you an observer's perspective. Do you notice the change in your feelings?

If you want to get an extra boost, you can imagine floating outside of your body, looking at yourself, and then getting back into your body again to look at yourself while you are looking at yourself. The double dissociation will get rid of the negative emotion or at least make it so minor that you can deal with it.

There are guided audios that you can use to help you with this technique, and most of them use imagery and hypnotic language as well to help you to handle overwhelming feelings like phobias, anger, fear, sadness, grief, and jealousy.

In essence, three things are critical to making an enduring change:

- You have to be tired enough of dealing with the same problem over and over until that drives change
- You have to change the perspective through which you see the problem so that you see it in a new light
- You have to come up with an appealing option that will be worthy enough for you to pursue

The simplest way to go about it is to change your perspective. There is a common expression that 'you can't see the forest for the trees' used to describe someone who is too involved in the details of a problem to see the situation as a whole. When you are in the moment, it is easy to be too close that you see nothing else but the trees. Back up and view yourself as you have the experience. That way, you dissociate from it.

You allow your mind to give you another viewpoint. You are an observer. This is a powerful technique that you can use any time you like. You have to be careful, though, that you do not shove emotions into the shadow. The point is not to become emotionless but to process the emotions and to introduce options.

Dissociation helps to deal with the delusion that you are your sadness or that you are your anger. When you are stuck in the feelings, and you become the feeling, it will be difficult for it to ever change – the process is called nominalizing, and it is one of the biggest problems that people face.

The dissociation technique helps you to see 'the forest even as you are facing the trees' and to set yourself free of overwhelming emotions. However, it takes courage to do this technique and do it well. For a moment, it will cause you to experience deep feelings which many people are afraid of, but it will help you if you take the time to do that. Before you begin, think of a negative experience or feeling that is persistent that you would like to change forever.

Content Reframing

Try content reframing when you start to feel that a situation is helpless and negative. Reframing will remove the negativity in the situation and will empower you by changing the meaning that you assign to the experience into something positive.

For instance, say a relationship you care about has just ended. This on the surface may seem awful, but there are ways to reframe it so that it is bearable. Ask questions like: Are there benefits to being single? You now have many options when it comes to potential relationships. You also get the freedom to do the things you want when you feel like doing them. You can even think about the lessons you have learned from the relationship that would help you to have better relationships in the days to come.

In circumstances that you were expecting something bad to happen, it is easy to feel afraid and to focus on that fear, but that only causes more problems. You can instead focus on the responsibility you have to yourself. That way, you empower yourself to get out of the situation.

Essentially, content reframing is about assigning a different meaning by re-examining past experiences. It is going back to an event in your mind and finding alternative explanations to events that you find disturbing. It helps you to implement new desired behaviors or to get over hurtful words that were said about you.

It is vital to note that reframing in life happens

regardless of NLP. Conscious or not, your brain will create meaning and assign them to different events. Context framing is about choosing to assign a meaning that works for your betterment.

A frame offers a context or a focus for your actions and thoughts. The way the frame in a picture puts boundaries and borders on what you see in the picture, a frame of reference helps you live out your beliefs and to know how to interact with others and with yourself. It lets you see what your perceived role in life is and your perceived skills, abilities, and limitations. People are constantly setting frames, limits, and boundaries on the things you can do and those you cannot do, and they sometimes do this without thinking about the truthfulness of the limitations and their consequences.

Changing the frame when you have had an experience can influence a lot the way that you perceive, react, and interpret the experience. If you are told that you have just one hour to finish a task, that will cause you to be anxious and may stand in the way of doing that task well, affecting the quality as opposed to if you had a whole week to complete the same task. This is an illustration of how one detail in the frame can impact the choices that you make.

Reframing is about improving your experience and hence improving your actions to see the impact of your beliefs. It is more resourceful than any choice that you may make in your reaction.

When trying to reframe content, ask yourself questions such as: What other meaning could this event have? In what ways could this prove to be a resource or a positive experience?

When you reframe the content or the meaning of an event, you are choosing the specific aspects that you will focus on. You can, for example, see an electrical power failure as a disruptive occurrence and a disaster given everything you have to do, or you can see it as an opportunity for you to spend quality time with your loved ones and to have fun in innovative ways.

You can use content reframing for statements like, 'I get angry when my boss hovers as I work.' Do you see how the persona has taken an event and assigned meaning to it? Granted, the association could be true; it also limits how resourceful the person is and what they can do in such instances. To reframe the situation, think about the underlying assumption of NLP that 'each behavior action has a positive intent.'

Ask yourself questions like: What is your boss looking to achieve with this behavior? Why does he do it? Is there a positive value in his actions? The positive value could be on the side of the boss or the employee in this case. You could reframe the situation like: 'it is a good thing that you know your boundaries well enough and are unwilling to let people violate them.'

Content reframing is about finding the lessons in every experience and finding meaning in life.

Anchoring Yourself

Anchoring came from a Russian scientist, Ivan

Pavlov, who experimented with dogs. He rang a bell repeatedly every time the dogs were eating. After repeating the experiment for a while, he could ring the bell and have the dogs drooling regardless of the time, even if there was no food available.

The action created an association between the behavior of eating and the bell – conditioned response.

With this NLP technique, you can use stimulus-response anchors to form habits.

Anchoring will help you to form associations between a positive emotional response that you desire and a specific sensation or phrase. When you pick a positive thought or emotion and connect it deliberately to a gesture, you can make it an anchor to use anytime you feel low to change your feelings immediately.

To anchor yourself, identify a feeling you want to experience, whether it be calmness, confidence, or happiness. Find a place on your body where you would like to anchor the emotion. It could be with a simple action like squeezing a fingernail, pulling an earlobe, or touching a knuckle. It does not matter where you pick, just as long it is a place that is unique enough that you are not constantly touching it.

Think back to a time in the past when you felt the state that you want. Go back to that time mentally and float into your body. Look through your eyes and relive the memory. Be careful to adjust your body language so that it matches that state and memory. Tour through the things you saw, listen for thing things you heard, and feel what you remember feeling. You will start to enter into that state. This step compares to recounting a funny story from the past to your friend and as you get into it more, you laugh again because of the associations to the story that allow you to relive it.

As you inhabit the memory, squeeze, touch, or pull the body area that you chose. As you relive the memory, your brain will make associations between the memory and the gesture. Release the touch when the emotional peak begins to wear off. This will form a stimulus-response that will trigger the state every time you make that touch. To feel it, you just have to touch yourself that same way.

If you want to strengthen the response, you can

think of another memory where you felt the same state. Return and relive it through your eyes. Anchor it on the same spot. Whenever you add a memory, the anchor gains potency, and the response it will trigger will be stronger. You can use this technique whenever you want to change your mood.

Anchoring is fundamental in NLP and can help you feel more enthusiastic, confident, and relaxed as you meet new people.

It is an easy way to let you change unwanted feelings to resourceful feelings in moments. When you create an anchor, you create a stimulus-response pattern to allow you to feel however you want, whenever you want.

In essence, you associate an internal response

to an external trigger so that it can happen fast and often covertly. The association is considered reflexive, and not something you choose.

In NLP, anchoring has been expanded to include some connections between other experiential aspects beyond the behavioral responses and environmental cues. A remembered photo, for example, could become an anchor for a specific feeling. A tone of voice could also become an anchor for a state of confidence or excitement. A person could consciously decide to create and re-trigger the associations instead of them being a mindless and knee-jerk reflex. That way, you use an anchor as a tool for self-empowerment. Anchoring can help to establish and reactivate mental processes associated with learning, creativity, and concentration.

Rapport

The dictionary definition of rapport is a relationship marked by conformity, affinity, and harmony. It supports alignment, agreement, and similarity.

NLP rapport is the ability to relate to others or make them feel like you do in a way that will create understanding and trust. It is the ability to see beyond your perspective into the other person's and to have them understand yours. You do not have to agree with the perspective they have, and you do not have to like it. This technique makes any communication easy.

There are many ways to build rapport, but one of the fastest and most effective ways comes from NLP. In this technique, you subtly mirror the other person's body language, words, and tone of voice.

People are drawn to others who are like them. By mirroring the other person subtly, their brain will fire off mirror neurons and pleasure sensors to make them like you.

This technique is easy; sit or stand the way a person is standing and tilt your head the way that they have. When they smile, smile as well, and mirror their facial expression. When they cross their legs, cross yours and imitate their voice.

You have to be subtle when trying to create rapport. If you do the activities overtly, the other person will consciously notice, and that breaks rapport, so be sure to mirror calmly and naturally.

A successful interaction hugely depends on people's ability to establish and keep rapport. In fact, more business decisions are made based on rapport than technical merit of the business. You will likely make purchases from people you agree with and offer support to a person that you can relate with than someone you find it hard to understand.

NLP rapport techniques are powerful in their effects and implications. There are two ways that you can learn to view other people. You can choose to emphasize what you have that is not common, or you can zoom in on the similarities. You can always figure out a thing or two that you share with a person, even if it is your humanity. In the same way, you will always have differences with other people.

When you zero in on the differences, establishing rapport becomes difficult. By dwelling on the things that you have in common, antagonism and resistance disappear, and cooperation improves. The good news is that as you practice, it becomes easier to identify the things you have in common with others and to focus on those.

A significant feature of NLP rapport is pacing. Pacing is what maintains that rapport. By definition, it is the process of moving the way the other person moves. In doing so, you accept their behavior and set them up as a model for existing in the world. Rapport is concerned with reducing the perceived or real differences at an unconscious level.

You can pace different aspects of behavior, as

you saw in the examples given earlier. Note that if the other person catches on to what you are doing, it can become awkward – any obvious attempts of imitating will break the harmony. Pacing has to be unconscious. After rapport has been established, you can influence the behavior of the other person. One way to confirm rapport is that when you make a movement, the other person follows you. For example, if you scratch your nose or yawn, they will do the same.

Matching happens naturally in some contexts. Watch someone as they have a conversation with a small child. They will likely crouch to get to the height of the child and will talk excitedly or slowly based on the situation. In restaurants, romantic couples often appear engaged in some sort of dance as they lean and smile at each other in mirroring postures.

To create rapport, you can also adjust your whole body, a part of it, or half of it to match the other person. You can match the poses they offer with their shoulders or head. However, if the body posture is unusual, do not match it, or it will seem disrespectful. You have to be subtle.

You can also match other aspects like voice and breathing. You can match the rate of a person's breathing or the depth of it, just as long as you do not do it to a person with difficulty breathing. As for the voice, match the pitch, volume, pace, type of words, and tone. This may be difficult to learn, but it will be worth it when you do. You do not have to match everything; you can just choose one. If a person speaks slowly, slow your speech down as well. If they speak softly, drop the volume in your voice.

You can create rapport by authentically trying to understand another person's values and beliefs without judging them. It is important to remember that the goal is not to change their values, agree with them, or even dispute; it is to understand.

The final aspect that you can match is the language pattern. Many people in the marketing and sales sectors match language patterns. Here, you use the same words to describe processes and things so that the person feels understood.

Persuasion and Influence

A lot of the work in NLP is dedicated to helping people get rid of their negative emotions, bad habits, and limiting beliefs. Influence and persuasion are about changing the way people do or perceive things ethically. They help you to deal with the contribution of relationships to a positive mindset as earlier discussed and can be thought of as a way to manage relationships.

One of the major contributors to the field, Milton Erickson, was a psychiatrist who studied the subconscious mind and used hypnotherapy to understand it. He had mastered hypnosis to the point that he found a way to communicate with the subconscious minds of other people outside of hypnosis. It is said that he could hypnotize people anywhere and anytime in normal conversations. His methods of hypnosis were later developed to be called conversational hypnosis.

Conversational hypnosis can be used to persuade and influence people and to help them to get over their fears, conflict, and limiting beliefs. It is useful for reaching people who are resistant.

Use the following tips to influence and persuade people:

- Framing – This is a technique that is common in politics. A common example is the inheritance tax. Politicians fighting the tax call it the 'death tax'. The term 'death' instead of 'inheritance' causes people to make negative associations with it. Framing is not obtrusive, but using emotive words can convince people to accept your perspective.

- Reflection – Reflecting is imitating the movements someone makes. It happens unconsciously, but you can do it intentionally. Try to be imperceptible and reflect them at intervals of two to four seconds between movements.
- Deficit – This technique is common with advertisers. Opportunities are more attractive if they have limited access or limited time offers. For example, free shipping, discount code, or a free gift that's available for a limited time only. This method works if you use it appropriately, but you have to stay on your guard. Think about how the technique will affect you as well.
- Interchange – When someone does something nice for you, you feel compelled to reciprocate. The idea here

is to do something nice for people you would like something from. No matter who it is, be sure to take the initiative first.

- Timing – People are usually more flexible and docile when they are tired. Before asking something of someone, you can bide time until they have exerted considerable mental effort. Catching a colleague at the end of the day could mean that no matter what you ask, they will promise to do it the next day.

- Congruence – Everyone is subconsciously trying to be consistent. An example of this technique is with sellers. A seller will likely shake hands as you negotiate a purchase. Most people make associations of that with the completion of a deal. Shaking hands before a sale is complete increases the chances that you will agree with the seller. You can use this technique to persuade people to do something before their logical mind comes alive.

- Smooth speech – In normal conversation, people will use phrases and exclamations to express uncertainty, like 'hmm' or 'well'. These words make you sound less convincing. Try to speak without them, and you will sound more confident and persuasive.
- Authorities and friends – You are likely to convince others to follow things that are important to you if you consider an authority.

Summary

NLP techniques are a user manual for the brain. They are tools to help you to take control of your thoughts and your feelings. They work by begging questions whose natural answer is a positive outlook.

From this chapter, you have learned how to use:

- Dissociation – the ability to step away from a situation so that you see the big picture and then align yourself properly
- Content framing – grabbing the lesson in a situation by shifting the perspective
- Anchoring – associating an action with a feeling or thought so that you can access it with a simple step when you need it

- Rapport – relating to other people in ways that reduce the visible differences between you
- Persuasion and influence – using techniques to ethically convince people to adopt a different mode of being or doing things

Chapter 7: Daily Rituals for a Positive Mindset

Why Rituals are Important

Your future is not shaped by the major events or decisions in your life but by your daily habits. What you do every day; the choices you make define who you become. That is the place of rituals. They give you a sense of control.

In this chapter, rituals are not religious ceremonies or obsessive-compulsive habits; they are practical things you do every day. Imagine going for a first date or a job interview; do you feel anxious? When the situation ahead of you is uncertain, rituals help you to focus.

They increase your performance by making small mundane acts significant and bringing with them joy and meaning.

When you are looking to change your mindset, nothing you do will work if you do not pour your heart into it. Rituals are symbolic acts that will help you engage your emotions. According to Bronislaw Malinowski, you turn to rituals when the outcome you want is important, outside of your control and uncertain.

The point is that even if rituals are associated with maintaining the status quo, the repetition has a significant effect beyond appearing a certain way to others. Rituals have been used in many cultures to deal with grief or increase confidence and reduce anxiety. They do not need to be communal. In the case of changing your mindset, rituals will likely be private and personal.

Rituals will shape how you perceive yourself. They will boost your self-confidence by improving focus and execution. This is the reason professional athletes, for example, will have a set of activities they perform before a competition.

When things are challenging, rituals can help to kill procrastination. They lower your anxiety levels and help you start a project you would otherwise leave untouched. They build a positive mindset and propel action.

Habits versus rituals

Rituals are different from habits in that you do not think about habits. You brush your teeth every day without having to think about it. By the time you are an adult, the behavior of brushing teeth daily has become automated. The difference with rituals is that they will increase mindfulness.

By definition, rituals are actions whose symbolic meaning goes past their instrumental value. The folding of the American flag is a ritual – it is not about showmanship or easy storage, but the folds have symbolic meaning. A ritual is a celebration that involves your full attention and emotions.

Rituals are specific and detailed. They are easy to repeat and help towards attaining a particular outcome. A ritual helps you prepare for something while a habit is done repeatedly to perform the action in question. You develop a habit without knowing, but you perform rituals deliberately. Rituals require engagement and intent.

Where a habit involves a specific action done repeatedly, a ritual involves many activities and elements – many habits. For example, Mark Twain would enter his study every morning and write until 5 pm. He skipped lunch and did not accept interruptions. After dinner, he would read the work he wrote that day to his family.

Habits are action-oriented – you start them and then keep doing them thoughtlessly. Rituals, on the other hand, are system-oriented. A ritual needs a clear beginning, middle, and end. When rituals become habits, it is because they have a deep meaning for the people involved.

Living within many ritual cycles is vital for your mental health. It helps to deal with feelings of anxiety and destabilization and allows you to create a clear path ahead.

Morning Rituals

Marcus Aurelius is credited with the quote 'When you wake up in the morning, consider the privilege of life – to think, to breathe, to enjoy and to love. '

Generating that positivity in the morning is a sure way to secure any day. In the precious hours of the morning, you set a mindset to carry you throughout the day, so it is vital to treat this period with respect and attention.

Create time to make your morning mindful by creating simple rituals that you can perform in a short time. The idea is to ease into the morning with purpose so that you create an open mind and a clear head to make sure that your day is full of direction, enthusiasm, and positive energy.

Bear in mind that you do not have to adopt all the rituals listed here; you can simply pick a couple that work for you and ensure that you do them consistently enough for them to become a habit.

- Practice gratitude

You can set an attitude of gratitude as you start your day by having a mindset that shows respect and appreciation for what you have and what will happen. Recognizing such emotions will bring more awareness of life. Gratitude is a self-inventory of thankfulness. You can practice it by keeping a gratitude journal. There, note down every morning up to five things that you are grateful for. Once in a while, you can also write gratitude letters to people you care about.

- Meditate

Consistent meditation practices will help you to reduce your stress levels and improve concentration. Meditating in the morning will increase self-awareness and start your day on the right foot. It will increase your happiness, productivity, and performance. If you are just starting, try concentration meditation or mindfulness meditation for five minutes every day. Focus on the thoughts entering your mind and how they influence your emotional state.

- Visualization

Entrepreneurs, top athletes, and highly driven people use visualization. Practicing visualization in the morning will help you to connect your emotions with your long-term and short-term goals. Emotions influence your state of mind and your state of mind will hugely affect the activities you do every day and their outcomes. When visualizing, you want to align the what, how, and why's of your life. It is critical that as you progress towards your goals, you refine and re-evaluate your vision. Feeling good about what you envision is paramount and will help you to keep on track.

- Affirmations

Affirmations are statements that influence your

mind to become goal-oriented. It affects your thinking, which in turn affects your behavior, habits, and performance. You can use affirmations to support your visualization activities or use them independently, provided you practice affirmations every morning. It is a plus if the statements align with your vision. Think of the affirmations as the "new codes" that you input into your program. Your subconscious mind takes in the positive statements and gradually uses that to re-condition yourself.

There are different techniques that you can do to increase the effects of your affirmations. First, use the words "I am" or "I choose" at the very start. Don't begin with, "I hope," "I wish," or "I want." These phrases are not as powerful and as confident as "I am" because they entail some levels of uncertainty. Formulate your affirmations with conviction. With that said, create them in such a way that it speaks to the present you. To what you are now. For example, 'I am strong and able to deal with whatever comes at me,' or 'I am beautiful and independent.'

- Exercise

Exercising in the morning can help you to get your day started well. It can set the tone for a healthier day and a happier mindset. When you exercise in the morning, you release cortisol, the hormone that keeps you alert and awake. Typically, the hormone increases in the morning and drops in the evening. Your body is primed to exercise in the morning. Other benefits of exercising in the morning include more overall energy, better mood, and better focus. The cherry on top is that it will support weight loss and appetite control.

- Forgiveness

Every morning, think about the things that you are likely holding on to that other people did that you need to let go of. Forgiveness clears your vision and helps you to face the day without anger and resentment, weighing you down. As you forgive other people, be keen to forgive yourself for the decisions you have made that you no longer feel support your vision.

- Goal setting

You can set aside a few minutes every morning to think about the day and how you want to spend it. Consider everything that needs doing and how the daily activities line up with your overall goal. You want to make sure that as you prepare your to-do list, you are spending time on things that support your vision for your life.

- Listening to or reading uplifting content

Some people listen to inspiring or smart TED talks. Others read motivating articles, quotes, or books to encourage them. You can also choose to listen to a podcast or music that will refocus your mind on what you want to achieve. Pick content that will give you a positive outlook on life. It will open your horizons, which is just what you need as you begin your day.

Before Bed Rituals

After the day, you will need to establish some

rituals that will set you up to sleep well and to wake up in the right mood to do it all over again. A positive mindset is something you have to work for, and it may require discipline in the first couple of days, but keep at it. The following are rituals you can set up to do every day before bed:

- Write three things that went well and three that did not

The point here is to audit your day. Acknowledge everything that went right each day to keep yourself from dwelling on the negative and to monitor the progress that you are making. It is an exercise in gratitude. There is also value in writing what did not go right. It allows you to know the tweaks to make before any problems that might be brewing become disasters. It will enable you to make small improvements daily and to correct your course when there is still time. This exercise should not take more than ten minutes.

- Make a to-do list for the next day

You can make this list as part of your nightly or morning routine. The point is to get a sense of what the next day looks like before you start it. A concise and clear to-do list will give you purpose. If you do it before you go to bed, it will allow your mind to rest – you will not have to worry about the next day. It gives your subconscious mind an opportunity to think about ideas all night. Once you wake up, you will have a clear sense of what the day brings.

- Remove what you need for the next day

Some people cannot go to bed without firmly laying out their clothes for the next day and preparing lunch so that it is ready to grab. The little rituals work like rehearsals for the next day, and they help you to sleep well. Getting the tasks done is also helpful for people whose schedules are so busy that they do not have much time to spare.

The more you can do ahead of schedule, the more prepared you will be to focus on the truly important things of the day. It will allow you to have fewer hitches because you will be prepared before you leave.

- Soak in a bath or take a hot shower

The whole idea of bedtime routines is to allow you to de-stress and relax. There will be days that you will need some more help to calm down and loosen up. A shower or a bath can help with that. Immersion in water is therapeutic and will help you to detach from how hyper-connected technology makes everything feel. Water has a way of relaxing your mind, to make your thoughts fluid and crystallize your ideas.

- Take a walk

Some people cannot go to bed if they did not work out at night. If that is not your kind of thing, consider taking a walk. Walk at a mild pace so that it is relaxing rather than taxing. It will allow your body to unwind and your mind to cool down. It will also give you plenty of space to reflect and provide another perspective that could create new ideas. Allow your thoughts to wander as you stroll.

- Stretch

If you spend most of your days behind a desk, your joints can feel stiff, and your muscles could begin to cramp. You can integrate stretching into your nighttime routine to help you loosen up and get a good night's sleep. Find a quiet space in your home and relegate it to the stretches. Your body will thank you for it.

- Spend time with someone you love

Research shows that the habit of talking over your day with someone you love can help to de-stress, recharge, swap stories, and reflect. Talking about the things happening in your life helps to develop deep and lasting relationships. You can do this with a family member, friends, or partner. Your brain calms down from the reminder that you are loved.

- Meditate

Meditation will help your mind to be at peace after a chaotic day. It gives you perspective and space to calm down the racing thoughts that rob you of sleep. Note that it will take patience and consistency to master meditation. Your brain is used to distractions and may resist focus. Keep at it, and you will enjoy the rewards.

- Visualization

One of the traits that successful people share is their ability to visualize what success looks like to them. After understanding the place they want to be, they create that image firmly in their mind. When you do this before bed, you solidify your goal in your mind as you sleep. According to Napoleon Hill, this visualization should be your chief aim. It helps to clarify the purpose of your life. It also helps you to affirm the outcome you desire, your biggest dreams, and goals. Doing this before you sleep will activate your subconscious as you sleep. Keep a notepad next to the bed to write down good ideas when you wake up.

- Adequate sleep

Adequate sleep is vital to making sure that you are well equipped to handle the next day. Successful people make sure they rest well. They know that less than five hours of sleep will leave them exhausted, mentally drained, and grumpy. Sleep deprivation is also connected to stroke, heart disease, and high blood pressure.

The recommended amount of sleep by the National Sleep Foundation is between seven and nine hours every night for adults. Make it a habit to sleep nearly the same time every night so that your body can set up a sleep rhythm and make your sleep invigorating. If you keep to a pattern, your body will be used to it and will give cues when the time is right until you no longer struggle to fall asleep.

- Journaling

Stressing or worrying before bedtime can stop your body from winding down. If it always appears like you get ideas of things to do when you need to be in bed, you may consider journaling to redirect your mind. Journaling will help you capture the thoughts in your mind and to let go of the stress of the day. There is so much information to consume throughout the day, and it is vital to know how to process it. In your journal, write down any thought that comes to mind and any 'great' ideas you might have. Revisit them the next day and see if you think them so great.

In addition, try to answer these questions honestly:

1. What good thing did I do today?
2. What bad thing happened today because of my actions?
3. Can I forgive myself and leave it behind?

You can create other questions for yourself based on the things you value and answer them per day. They will help you to process the day and to see how you interacted with other people all through.

Additional Considerations

Here are a few additional bonus hacks that can add to a good night's sleep.

- Change how you think about sleep

What are the last things you think just before you get into bed? Have you ever thought to yourself that 'I am so exhausted, I will never get enough sleep?' Or perhaps you count the hours you have to sleep and consider them not to be enough. Remember that it is not just your thoughts about life in general that determine your destiny; even what you think about sleep can bring rest or trouble. Reframe your thoughts to positive thoughts and watch that change the way you live.

- Get rid of the blue light

Remove the blue light from the devices in the bedroom. Blue light affects your sleep negatively. Get rid of any alarm clocks or night lights that burn blue and avoid bringing phones and tablets into the bedroom.

- Turn the clock around

When you look at your clock, you start to worry about how little time you have to sleep. It is understandable but avoidable. A simple solution is to have the clock face the other direction.

- Create a different sleeping space for your pet

Animals get restless, and your pet can get in the way of you having proper rest.

Summary

In this chapter, you have learned what makes a ritual and how rituals are different from habits. Rituals are intentional and unite your emotions towards a specific goal. Repeated over time, they could become habits. When trying to develop a positive outlook, rituals will help you to stay focused. They will get rid of inaction and move you toward your goal.

Rituals transform the mundane and allow you to be more mindful. In the morning, start your day on the right foot by:

- Keeping a gratitude journal
- Forgiving yourself and others

- Exercising
- Setting goals
- Visualization
- Meditation and
- Affirming yourself

When the day ends, finish it in style by:

- Meditating
- Journaling
- Taking a walk
- Stretching
- Making a to-do list for the next day
- Planning what you need for the next day and
- Having adequate sleep

Develop a Positive Mindset and Attract the Life of Your Dreams

Chapter 8: Reaching Your Full Potential

"The only person you are destined to become is the person you decide to be." – Ralph Waldo Emerson

Have you ever felt like you are not living up to your potential? Or perhaps you are unsure whether it is even possible to reach your full potential. If that is you, it means that you are an ambitious person who wants to live their life the best way you know how. That is what it means to reach your potential.

Everyone's time on earth is limited. Some people live longer than others, but it is not about how long you live but what you do with the time you have. It is about living your dreams and aspirations. It is essential to clarify that in the context of this book, reaching your potential is not about living up to the society's or people's expectations of you.

When all is said and done, and you are alone with yourself, are you happy with the choices you have made? When you chase goals and objectives that are not yours (imposed) even if you succeed, your success will be empty.

Reaching your potential is about becoming the best version of yourself. That is the goal.

It is a beautiful thing to want to reach your full potential and to strengthen your abilities as much as you can. As a rule of thumb, think through whatever your goal is so that when you know your "why", you will be able to withstand anything that comes your way, including criticism and the judgment of people who do not even know you.

Guard what you believe success to look like from outside influences and from situations where you have to defend it unnecessarily, and remember that Rome was not built in one day. You will need to persist regardless of the unexpected events and setbacks and anything that resists your path. Reaching your potential will require tenacity.

Regardless of the success you have accumulated in life and no matter where you are at, you can always do better. Keep working and keep pushing forward after you hit the goal you are pursuing. With that in mind, the following are seven skills you will need to reach your full potential.

7 Skills to Reach Your Full Potential

1. Self-awareness

Self-awareness is about being comfortable with what you are and where you are in life. It is about giving up any pretenses and impulses to be anyone you are not. When you are self-aware, you do not change yourself simply because other people think you should.

To reach your full potential, you have to know who you are and be proud of it. If you are not aware, you can find out – write, think, talk, and read – they all help you to be mindful of what your thoughts are. When you are self-aware, you will learn more about who you are automatically. Self-knowledge accompanies self-awareness.

2. Leadership

Keep the focus on yourself and work on your problems. You want to become a person who is stable enough to rely on. When you have achieved that, your goal will now be to inspire others to put as much effort into their lives. The best way to do that is to teach people how they can rely on themselves. A leader teaches other people to be independent and sets a good example, and a narcissist wants dependents.

3. Effective communication

Better writing is inevitably connected to better thinking. Better thinking is connected to better communication, which then produces better results in every area of life. If you never thought writing to be important, you can change that now. Start working on improving your writing skills, if you want to express yourself better and begin making connections you never thought possible.

Diction refers to your natural manner of speaking and is a very powerful tool in any society. When interacting with others, it can determine your credibility in their eyes and even whether or not they like you. By working on your diction and speaking ability, you'll be able to speak clearly and with conviction, improve your charisma around others, and emerge as a more self-assured individual.

4. Assertiveness

All of us can think of times when we know we should speak up, but we don't. When we feel like we're being taken advantage of, but we just accept it. Later, we kick ourselves, thinking: "If only I would have said something!"

Being assertive will allow you to stand up for what you believe, ask for what you want and need, and say no to what you don't want in a way that's confident, calm, and respectful.

5. Goal setting

One of the common assumptions people make when they hear about mindfulness is that you will no longer have the drive to pursue goals. The reverse, however, is true. The more present you are, the more you feel compelled to improve your circumstances and to find ways to do that. Just thinking about achieving your goals will not achieve them for you – you have to do the work. You have to set the goals and take action.

Setting goals is about clarifying where you want to be in a specific period. After that, break down what it looks like to be there into activities to do every day. That will help with productivity. You will know what a productive day for you looks like, and the things that deserve your attention.

6. Perseverance

There will be many days that you will want to give up because you will not always see results. What do you do then? You keep working even without the money, recognition, or rewards. You plow ahead and trust the process. In due time, you start to enjoy the results of your hard work. Once this starts to happen, the benefits motivate you further, and you put more effort to reap even more of them in a cycle.

7. Self-development

The importance of self-development often goes unnoticed. We choose to conveniently brush our shortcomings under the carpet. Just as learning should never stop, the same applies to self-improvement. The idea should be to focus on continuous self-development at every stage in our lives and become better versions of ourselves. By choosing to take charge of our development, we are able to reach our full potential and move forward to achieve what we want.

The route to excellence is one of constantly developing oneself. You have to resolve that you will compete against yourself. If you did ten sit-ups in your work out this week, you do 12 the next. The idea is to keep becoming better than you were the previous day. Making that commitment to self-development is the first step on the path to personal fulfillment.

Dream, Believe, and Dare to Do

"In this world, you're either growing or you're dying, so get in motion and grow." –Lou Holtz

Some people believe that you reach your full

potential at a specific age. This means that at that age, you are the best you can be, and after that, you are unlikely to get better. Such people could frown at any effort to be better. They might tell you that you are too old to be putting in a certain amount of effort.

Society says that it is only young people who manage to get to their full potential and that the older you get, the fewer the chances you will have. However, this does not have to be true for you – it may be socially accepted, but you do not have to accept it as true.

You can change your life at any age – you do not have to be young to try to get to your goals. It is never too late to unlock your full potential.

There are numerous examples of successful

people who only achieved success when they were much older. Age is simply a number that you do not have to allow to hold you back from trying to be better. Think about the following examples:

- Martha Stewart worked in catering for many years before she began hosting her TV show. She started writing her books in her 40s.
- Before Henry Ford was successful, he worked as an engineer, being trained by Thomas Edison. He was 40 years of age when he founded the Ford Motor company.
- Warren Buffett has made 99.7% of his wealth after the age of 52
- Ray Kroc passed his 50th birthday before he bought the first McDonald's in 1961,

> which he ultimately expanded into a worldwide conglomerate.
- Sam Walton opened the first Wal-Mart in 1962 when he was 44.

One of the most critical factors to being successful is the belief that you can be successful. If you consistently put yourself down and convince yourself that you cannot reach your potential, the chances are that you will not.

You have to believe in the person that you are and the power you have to get over your limiting beliefs. You are the only thing that is holding you back. Not even the criticism and negative words of other people have that power to get in your way.

Alongside believing that you can reach your full potential, you have to believe also that you deserve the success of doing that. You have to replace any limiting beliefs you have with positive mindsets, so that no matter your age, you are motivated to change your habits and your lifestyle as you watch the negative beliefs fall off.

Dream, believe, and dare to do! You might be positively surprised at what comes out of your efforts.

Summary

Reaching your full potential will require you to put in a little more effort into your life. It will demand that you use skills like:

- Self-awareness

- Leadership
- Goal-setting
- Effective communication
- Mindfulness
- Self-development
- Perseverance

It will demand that you believe in yourself and in your ability to rise above any situation, to dare, to dream, and to do until you have the desires of your heart.

Develop a Positive Mindset and Attract the Life of Your Dreams

Conclusion

'*Optimism does not wait on facts; it deals with prospects.*' – Norman Cousins

Like optimism, a positive mindset is not a slave to the circumstances.

It could be the difference between success and failure, progress and stagnation in any area of your life. It can help you to avoid stress and to even out any devastating and challenging situation coming your way by allowing you to see the silver lining.

Every challenge becomes an opportunity for you to learn and to grow. You can accept reality and try to make the best of it. A positive mindset can help you to avoid mental and physical diseases. When you no longer give weight to the negative thoughts, your body does not experience the discomfort of worry, stress, frustration, and anxiety. According to research, there are undeniable connections between a stress-free life and a stronger immune system.

Most of the battles that you face in life can be won if you are confident in your abilities. When you have a positive mindset, confidence simply oozes out of you. You reconfigure your personality and perform at your best, which boosts your self-esteem and the knowledge that you can make the proper decisions at the appropriate time, confidently.

As demonstrated in this book, a positive mindset will benefit every area of your life and not just your career. Positivity is rooted in gratitude for the things you have, and it will always add happiness to those around you. By expressing appreciation and gratitude, you strengthen bonds and allow yourself to enjoy a satisfying life.

A positive attitude in life is an investment that continually pays off. You start by confronting things that get in the way of the mindset, leaning on techniques to do better, and developing daily rituals to cement it. Soon, a new attitude takes over, and you no longer have to think about it; it happens subconsciously.

It should be clear that achieving that positive attitude is not an impulse. There is no elixir, magic pill, or short cut towards changing your outlook. This is what makes the journey inherently rewarding. The icing on the cake is that a positively changed life is rooted in unlimited gratitude that you can practice for the rest of your life and whose benefits you will continue to reap.

It says a lot about how far you are in the process that you have chosen to read this book. You are well on your way to becoming a better you.

All the best in your efforts!

Develop a Positive Mindset and Attract the Life of Your Dreams

REFERENCES

1. *The Power of Positive Thinking.* (1956).
2. Gillespie, M.P. (1995). *The picture of Dorian gray: "what the world thinks me".* Macmillan Reference USA.
3. Emerson, R. W., & Tilton, E. M. (1939). *The letters of Ralph Waldo Emerson.* Columbia University Press.
4. Kolbert, E. (2014). *The sixth extinction: An unnatural history.* A&C Black.
5. Johnson, D.M (2011). Socrates and Athens. Cambridge University Press.
6. *12 ways to raise a competent, confident child with grit.* (2015, 5). Psychology Today. https://www.psychologytoday.com/us/blog/peaceful-parents-happy-kids/201506/12-ways-raise-competent-confident-child-grit
7. *Optimism may reduce risk of dying prematurely among women.* (2020, March 28). News. https://www.hsph.harvard.edu/news/press-releases/optimism-premature-death-women/

8. Santos-Longhurst, A. (n.d.). *How to think positive and have an optimistic outlook: 8 tips*. Healthline. https://www.healthline.come/health/how-to-think-positive
9. *What is positive mindset: 89 ways to achieve a positive mental attitude*. (2019, December 20). PositivePsychology.com. https://positivepsychology.com/positive-mindest/
10. 6. *Goal setting theory* – PSYCH 484: *Work attitudes and job motivation – Confluence. (n.d.). WikiSpaces* – Confluence. Retrieved July 12, 2020, from https://WikiSpaces.psu.edu/display/PSYCH484/6.+Goal+Setting+Theory
11. *Daily rituals: Create a positive mindset for a happier life. (n.d.)*. Liora. https://liorabels.com/daily-rituals-create-a-positive-mindset-for-a-happier-life/
12. *What mindset rituals do you do daily to improve the quality of your life?* (2018, January 19). Viral Solutions – Your Personal Chief Marketing Officer. https://viralsolutions.net/what-mindset-rituals-do-you-do-daily-to-improve-the-quality-of-your-life/#.XxUyG8gzbIV

13. *The power of rituals: How to build meaningful habits – Gustavo Razzetti.* (2020, February 25). Liberationist – Change Leadership. https://liberationist.org/the-power-of-rituals-how-to-build-meaningful-habits/
14. LeMind, A., & B.A. (2013, August 8). *8 simple techniques to persuade and influence people.* Learning Mind. https://www.learning-mind.com/8-simple-techniques-to-persuade-and-influence-people/
15. Lee, B. (1998). *The power principle: Influence with honor.* Simon &Schuster.
16. *8 tips for developing positive relationships.* (2013, March 21). Training Magazine/professionals. https://trainingmag.com/content/8-tips-developing-positive-relationships/
17. Anthony, K. (n.d.). *EFT tapping.* Healthline. https://www.healthline.com/health/eft-tapping
18. *7 essential beliefs for leadership success.* (2016, July 4). Leadership Freak. https://leadershipfreak.blog/2016/07/03/7-essential-beliefs-for-leadership-success/
19. Cre8veonline.com. (n.d.). *Anchoring – NLP technique: : NLP-secrets.com.* Upgrade Your

Mind with Neuro-Linguistic Programing (NLP), Body Language and Hypnosis. https://www.nlp-secrets.com/nlp-technique-anchoring.php

20. Gill, B. (2017, June 22). *New to visualization? Here are 5 step to get you started.* Forbes. https://www.forbes.com/sites/bhaligill/2017/06/22/new-to-visualization-here-are-5-steps-to-get-you-started/#5c8c80ef6e3f

21. Laozi, Wieger, L., Liezi, Zhuangzi, & Bryce, D. (1984). *Wisdom of the Daoist masters: The works of Lao Zi (Lao tzu), lie Zi (Lieh tzu), Zhung Zi (Chuang tzu).*

22. Gold, L. H., & Simon, R. I. (2015). *Gun violence and mental illness.* American Psychiatric Pub.

23. Johnson, R. A. (2009). *Inner work: Using dreams and active imagination for personal growth.* HarperCollins.

24. Hockenbury, D., & Hockenbury, S.E. (2012). *Discovering psychology.* Worth Publishers.

25. Darwin, C. (2013). *The expression of the emotions in man and animals.* Courier Corporation.

www.ingramcontent.com/pod-product-compliance
Lightning Source LLC
Chambersburg PA
CBHW020902080526
44589CB00011B/398